Miracle on Ice

written by
Joe Dunn

illustrated by
Ben Dunn

visit us at
www.abdopublishing.com

Published by Magic Wagon, a division of the ABDO Publishing Group, 8000 West 78th Street, Edina, Minnesota 55439. Copyright © 2008 by Abdo Consulting Group, Inc. International copyrights reserved in all countries. All rights reserved. No part of this book may be reproduced in any form without written permission from the publisher. Graphic Planet™ is a trademark and logo of Magic Wagon.

Printed in the United States.

Written by Joe Dunn
Illustrated by Ben Dunn
Colored by Wes Hartman
Lettered by Joe Dunn
Edited by Stephanie Hedlund
Interior layout and design by Antarctic Press
Cover art by Ben Dunn and Wes Hartman
Cover design by Neil Klinepier

Library of Congress Cataloging-in-Publication Data

Dunn, Joeming W.
Miracle on Ice / by Joe Dunn ; illustrated by Ben Dunn.
   p. cm. -- (Graphic history)
   Includes index.
   ISBN 978-1-60270-077-2
   1. Hockey--United States--History--20th century--Comic books, strips, etc.--Juvenile literature.
   2. Olympic Winter Games (13th : 1980 : Lake Placid, N.Y.)--Comic books, strips, etc.--Juvenile literature. I. Dunn, Ben, ill. II. Title.

GV848.4.U6D86 2008
796.9620973--dc22

                                                    2007006439

TABLE of CONTENTS

Chapter 1
Cold War..5

Chapter 2
Creating a Team...9

Chapter 3
Winter Games...15

Chapter 4
Tie Game...21

Chapter 5
Victory..25

Timeline..28

1980 U.S. Olympic Hockey Team.....................29

1980 USSR Olympic Hockey Team....................30

Glossary..31

Web Sites..31

Index...32

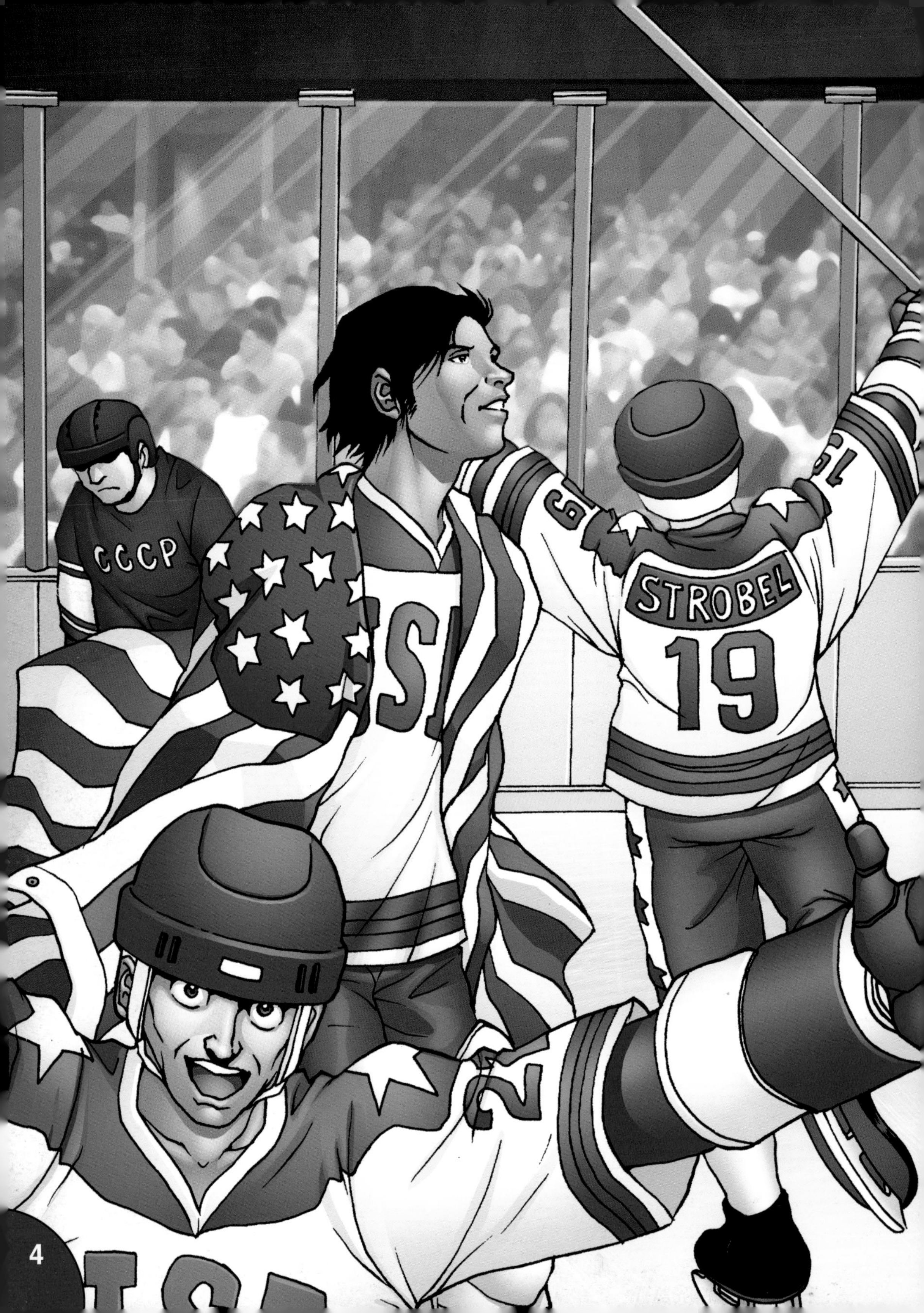
CCCP
STROBEL
19

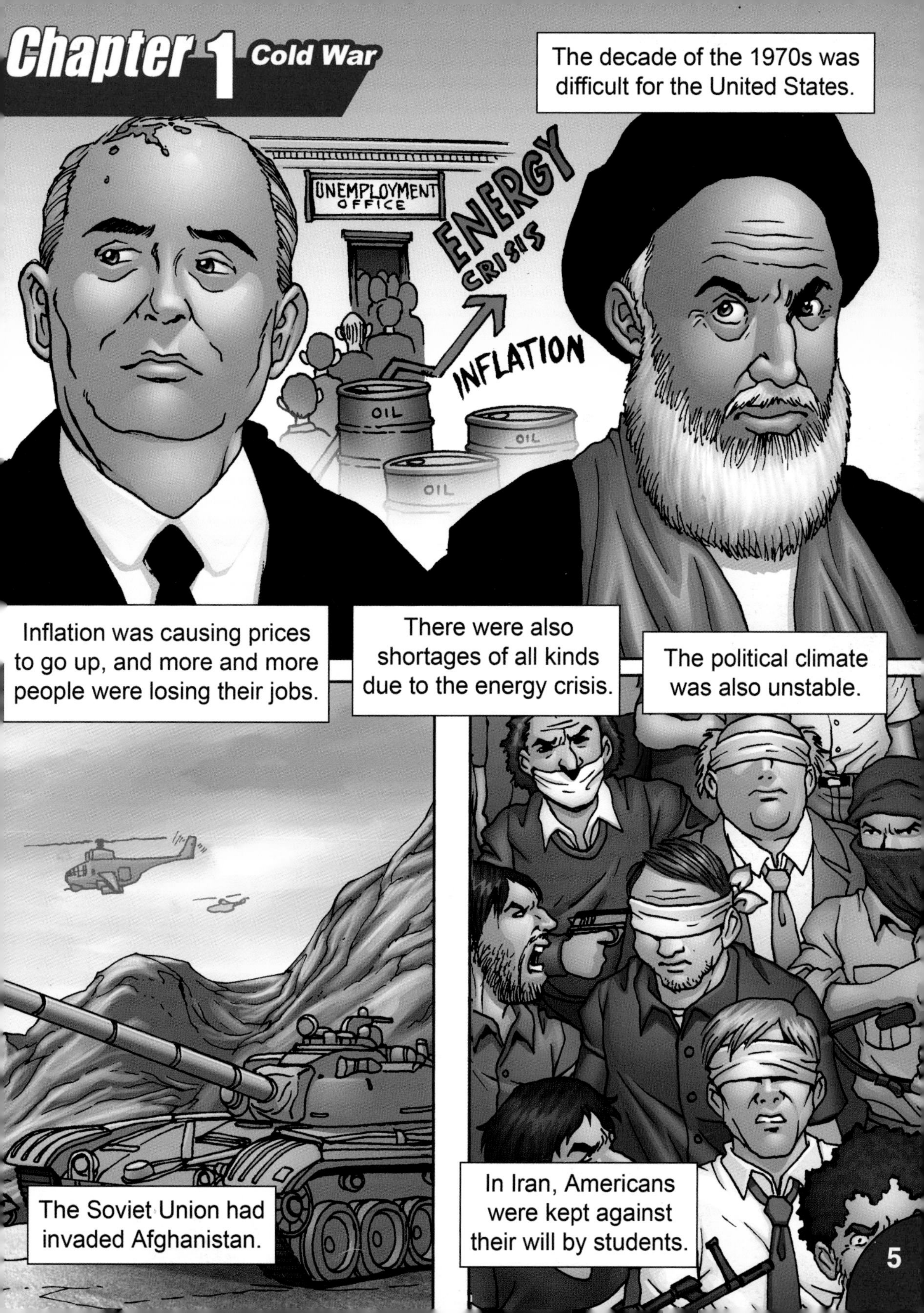
Chapter 1 Cold War
The decade of the 1970s was difficult for the United States.
UNEMPLOYMENT OFFICE
ENERGY CRISIS
INFLATION
OIL
OIL
OIL
Inflation was causing prices to go up, and more and more people were losing their jobs.
There were also shortages of all kinds due to the energy crisis.
The political climate was also unstable.
The Soviet Union had invaded Afghanistan.
In Iran, Americans were kept against their will by students.

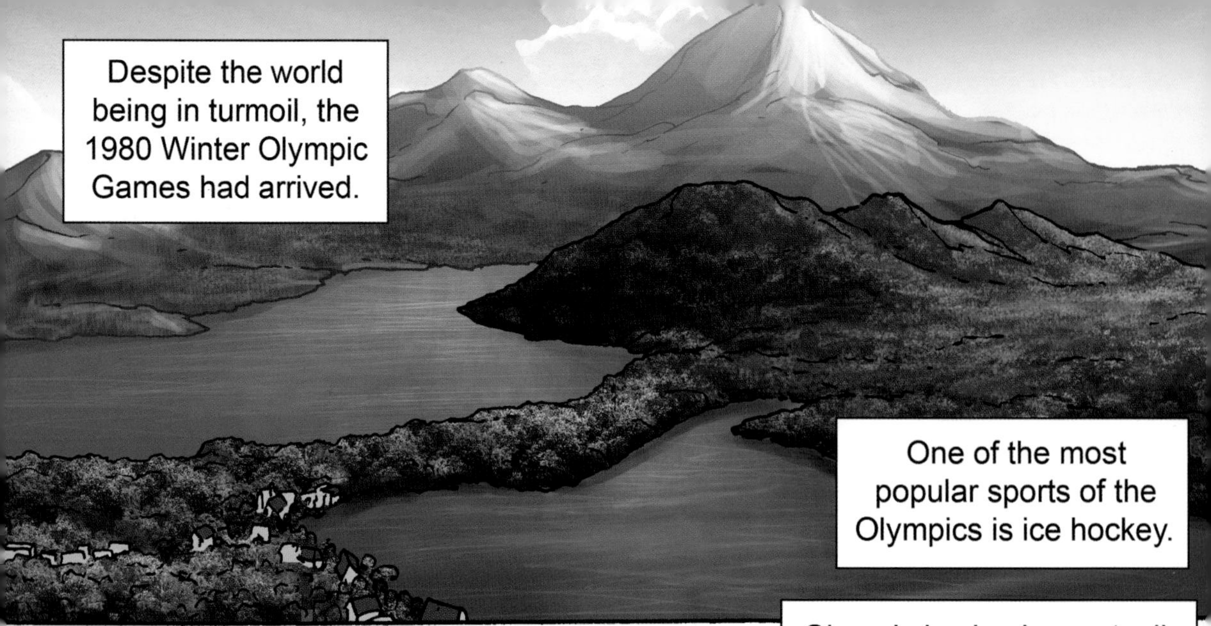
Despite the world being in turmoil, the 1980 Winter Olympic Games had arrived.
One of the most popular sports of the Olympics is ice hockey.

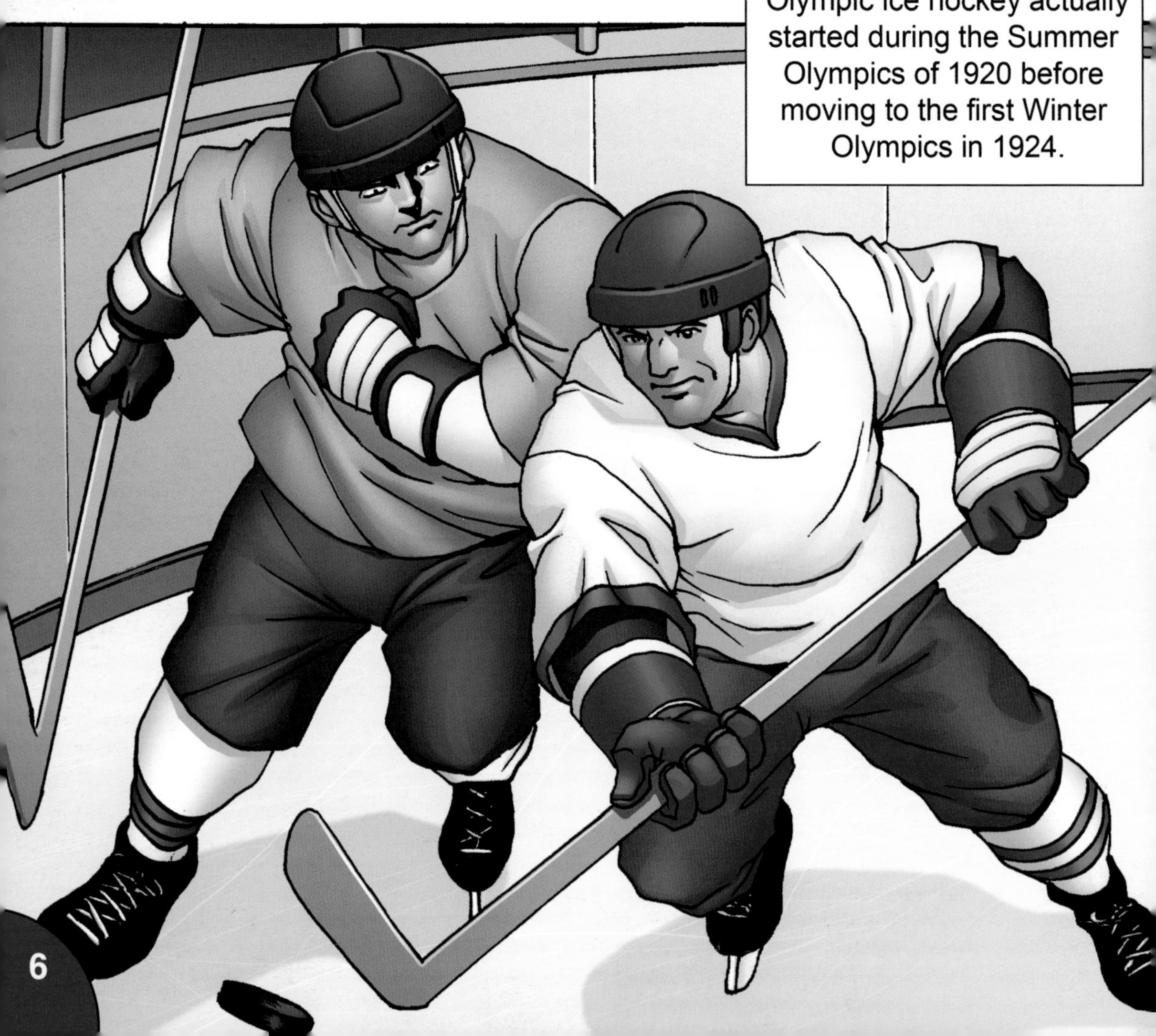
Olympic ice hockey actually started during the Summer Olympics of 1920 before moving to the first Winter Olympics in 1924.

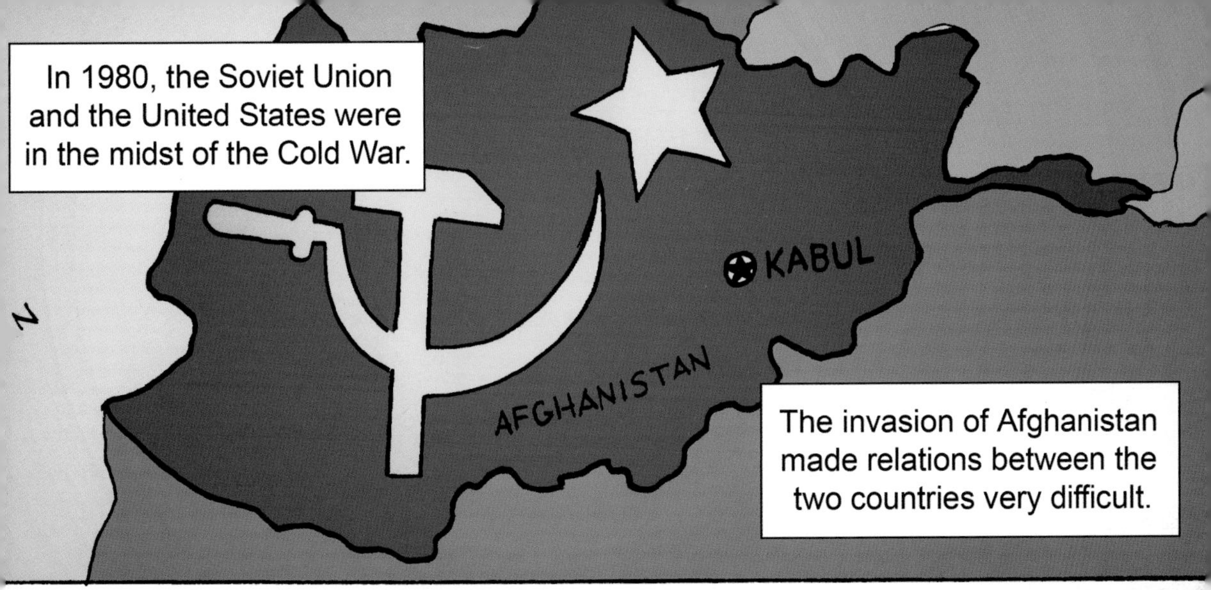
In 1980, the Soviet Union and the United States were in the midst of the Cold War.
N
KABUL
AFGHANISTAN
The invasion of Afghanistan made relations between the two countries very difficult.

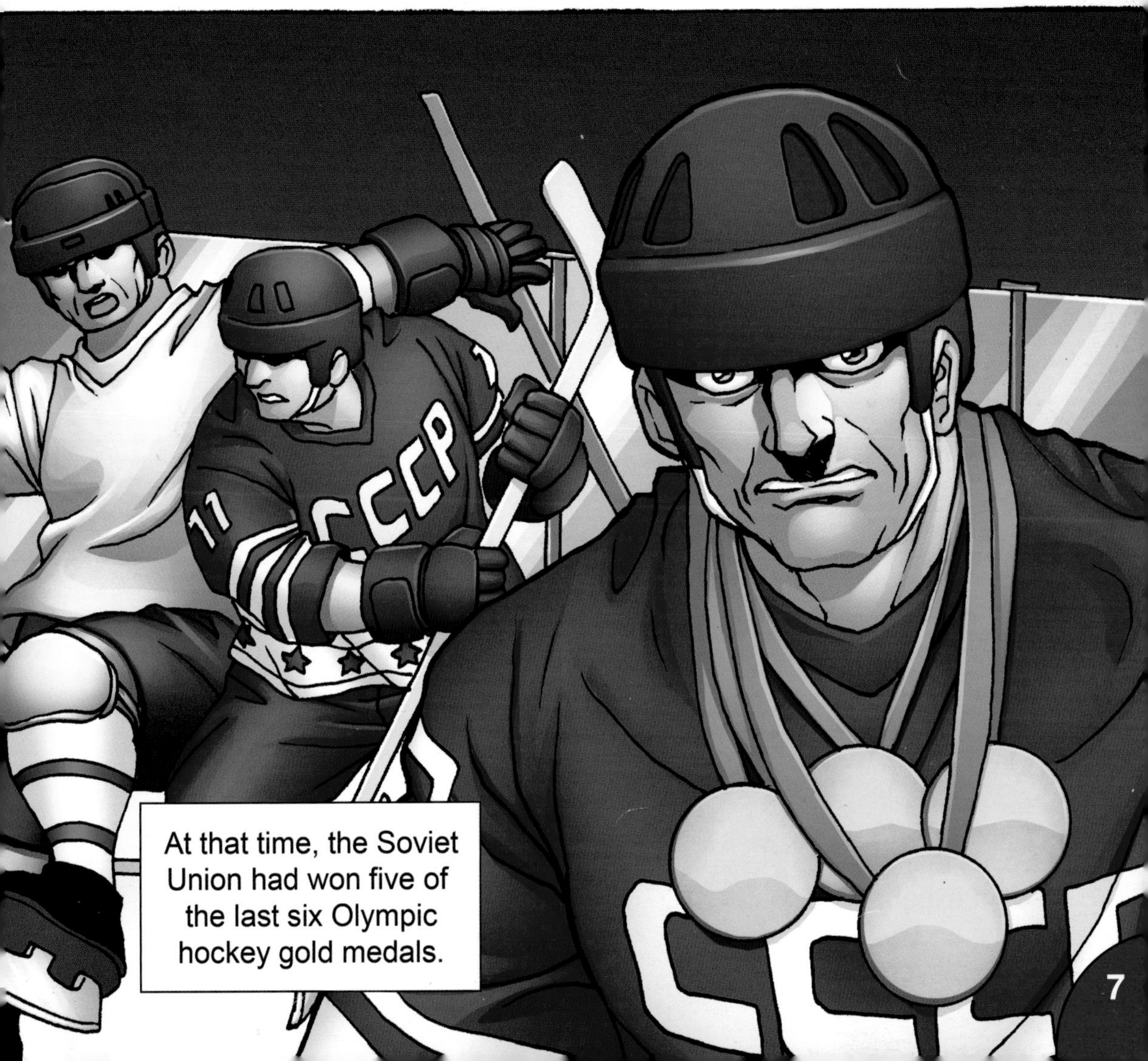
CCCP
11
At that time, the Soviet Union had won five of the last six Olympic hockey gold medals.

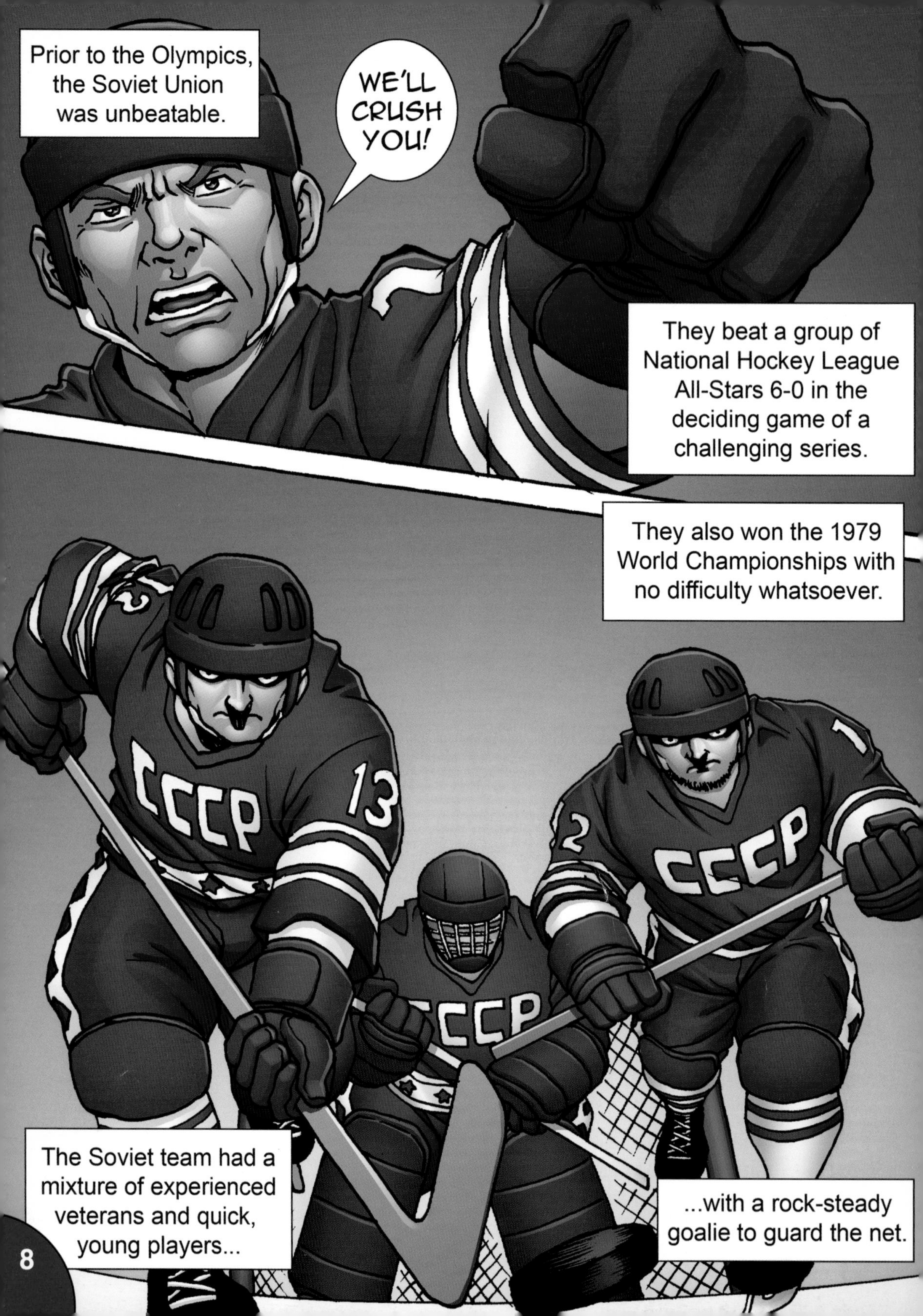

Prior to the Olympics, the Soviet Union was unbeatable.
WE'LL CRUSH YOU!
They beat a group of National Hockey League All-Stars 6-0 in the deciding game of a challenging series.
They also won the 1979 World Championships with no difficulty whatsoever.
CCCP
13
CCCP
2
1
CCCP
The Soviet team had a mixture of experienced veterans and quick, young players...
...with a rock-steady goalie to guard the net.

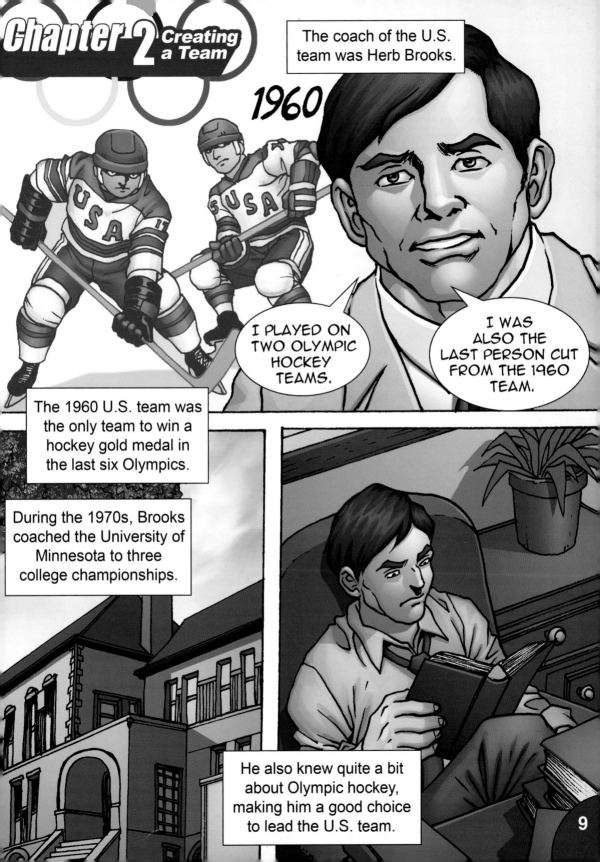

Chapter 2 Creating a Team

1960

The coach of the U.S. team was Herb Brooks.

I PLAYED ON TWO OLYMPIC HOCKEY TEAMS.

I WAS ALSO THE LAST PERSON CUT FROM THE 1960 TEAM.

The 1960 U.S. team was the only team to win a hockey gold medal in the last six Olympics.

During the 1970s, Brooks coached the University of Minnesota to three college championships.

He also knew quite a bit about Olympic hockey, making him a good choice to lead the U.S. team.

9

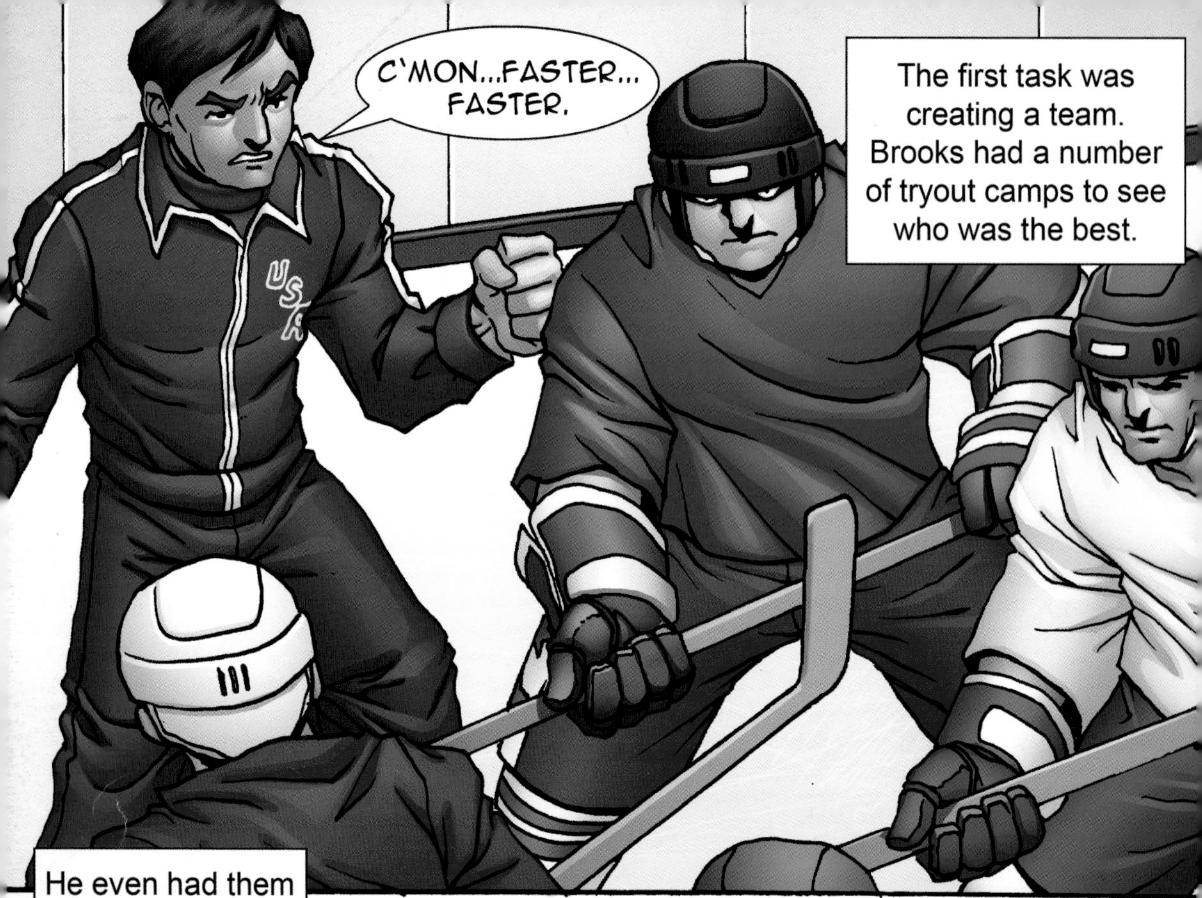
C'MON...FASTER... FASTER.
The first task was creating a team. Brooks had a number of tryout camps to see who was the best.

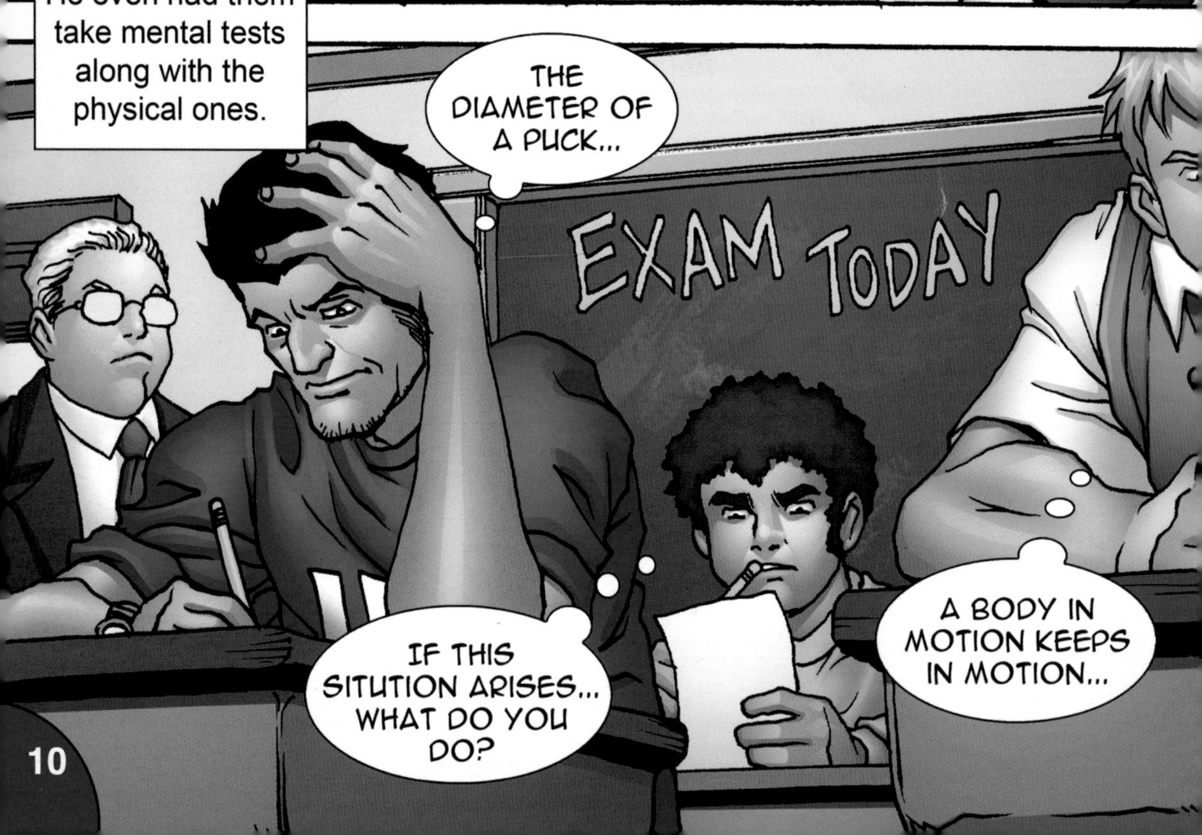
He even had them take mental tests along with the physical ones.
THE DIAMETER OF A PUCK...
EXAM TODAY
IF THIS SITUTION ARISES... WHAT DO YOU DO?
A BODY IN MOTION KEEPS IN MOTION...

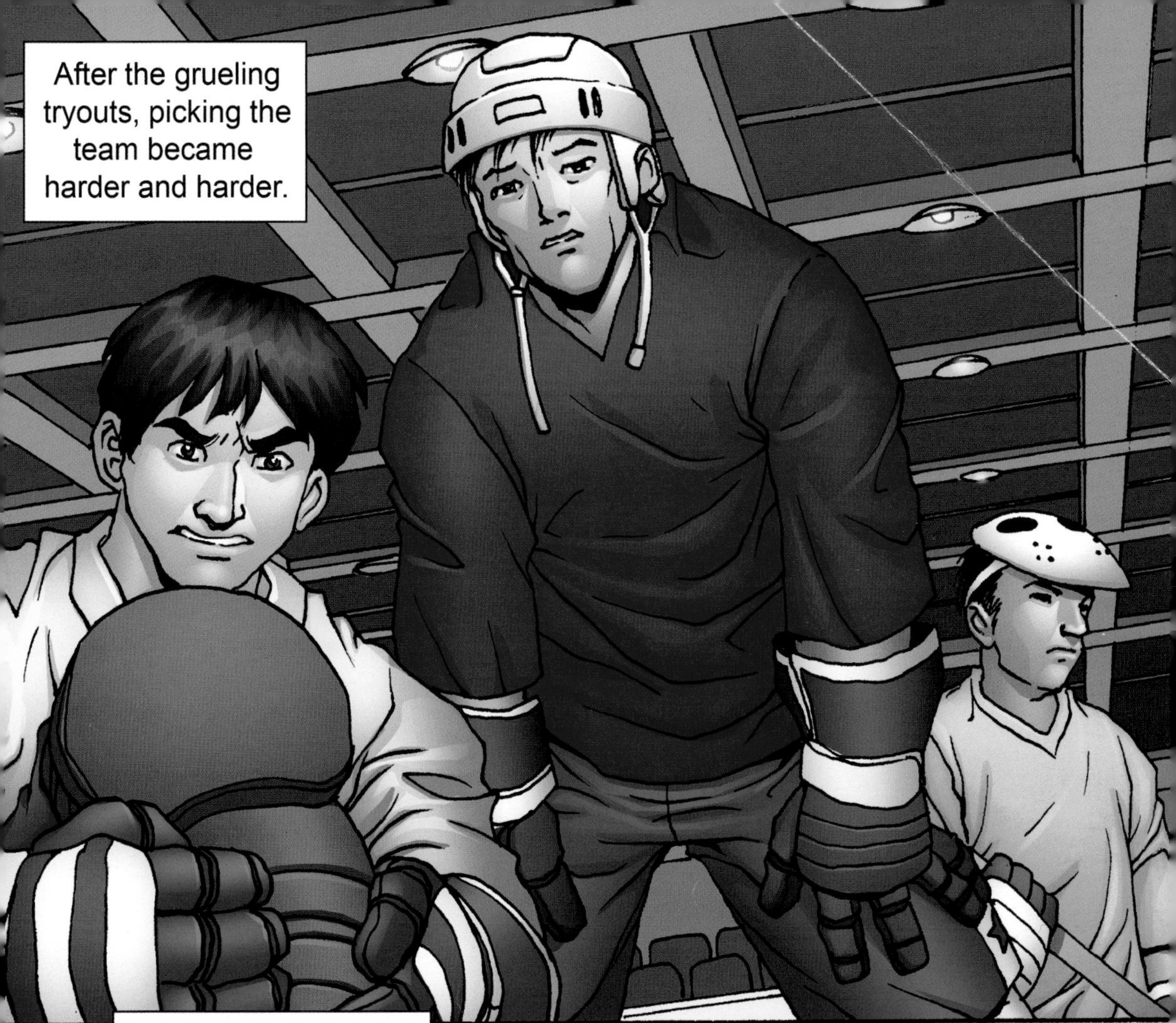
After the grueling tryouts, picking the team became harder and harder.

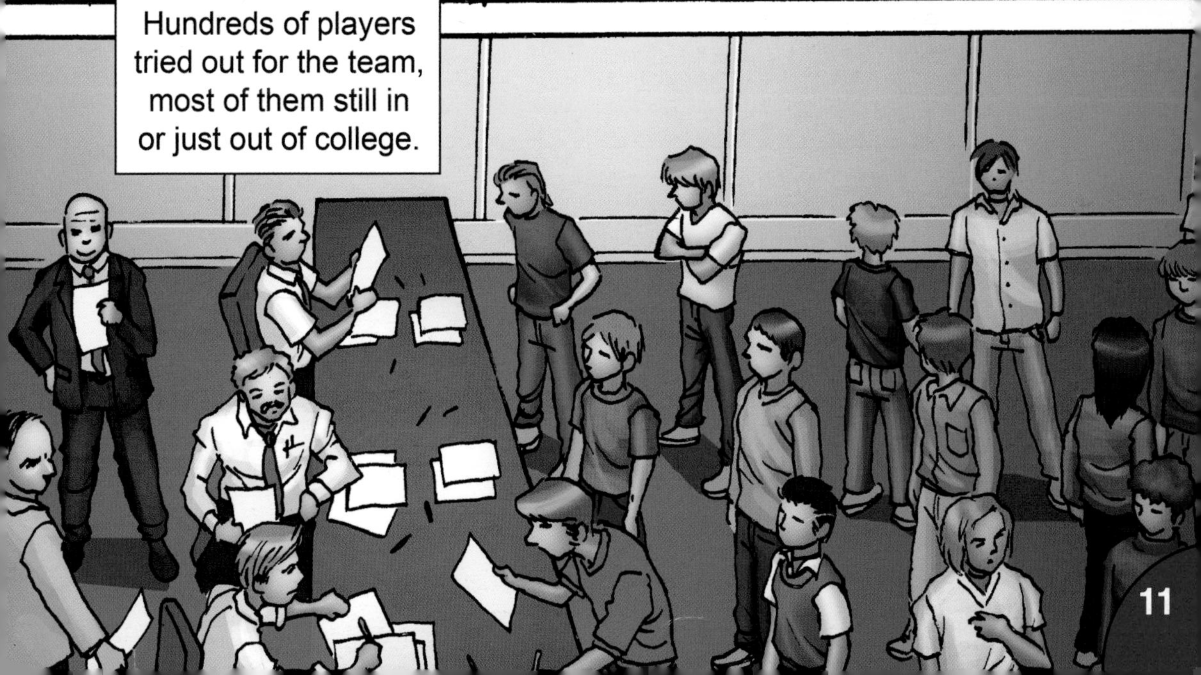
Hundreds of players tried out for the team, most of them still in or just out of college.

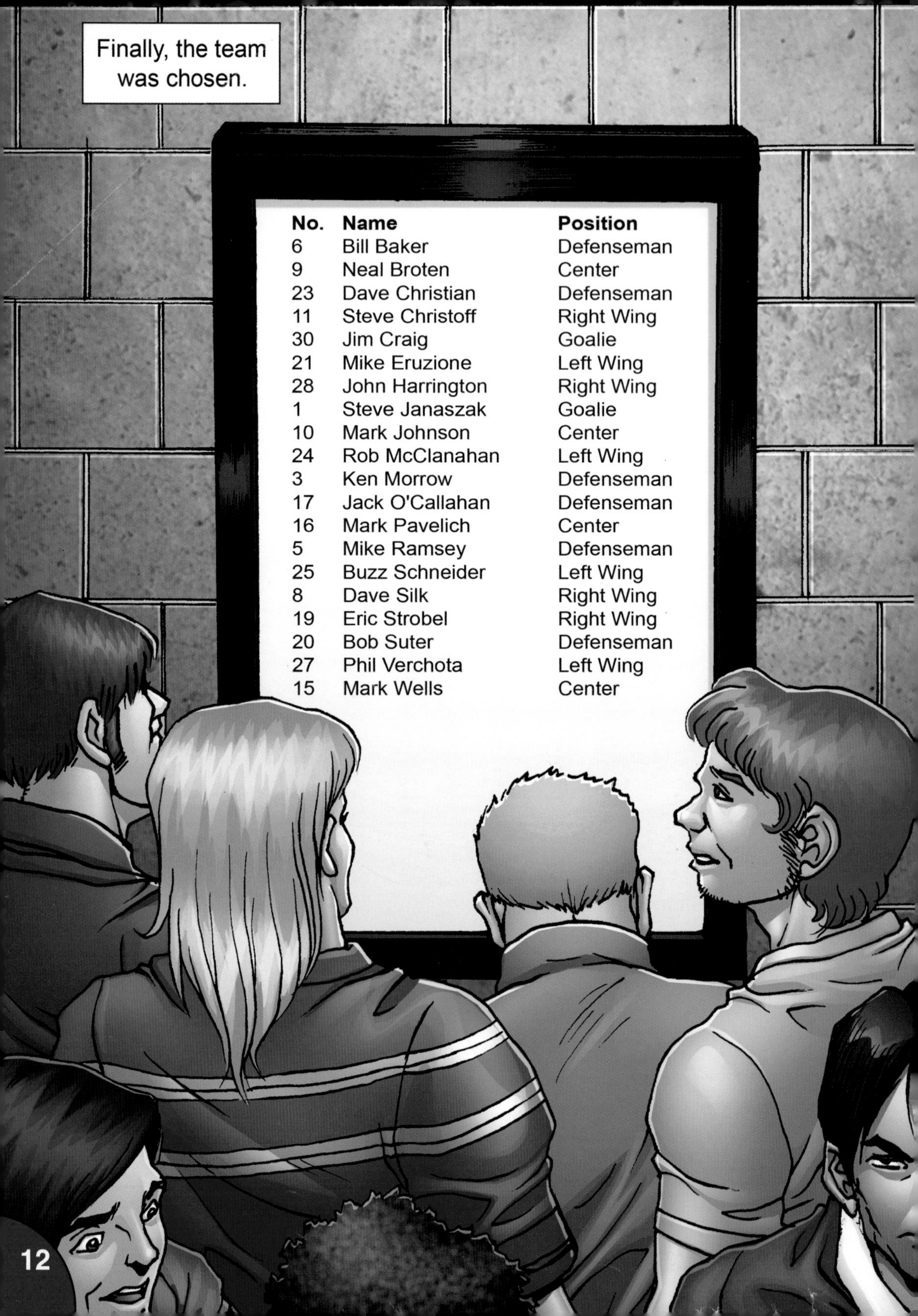
Finally, the team was chosen.
No. Name Position
6 Bill Baker Defenseman
9 Neal Broten Center
23 Dave Christian Defenseman
11 Steve Christoff Right Wing
30 Jim Craig Goalie
21 Mike Eruzione Left Wing
28 John Harrington Right Wing
1 Steve Janaszak Goalie
10 Mark Johnson Center
24 Rob McClanahan Left Wing
3 Ken Morrow Defenseman
17 Jack O'Callahan Defenseman
16 Mark Pavelich Center
5 Mike Ramsey Defenseman
25 Buzz Schneider Left Wing
8 Dave Silk Right Wing
19 Eric Strobel Right Wing
20 Bob Suter Defenseman
27 Phil Verchota Left Wing
15 Mark Wells Center

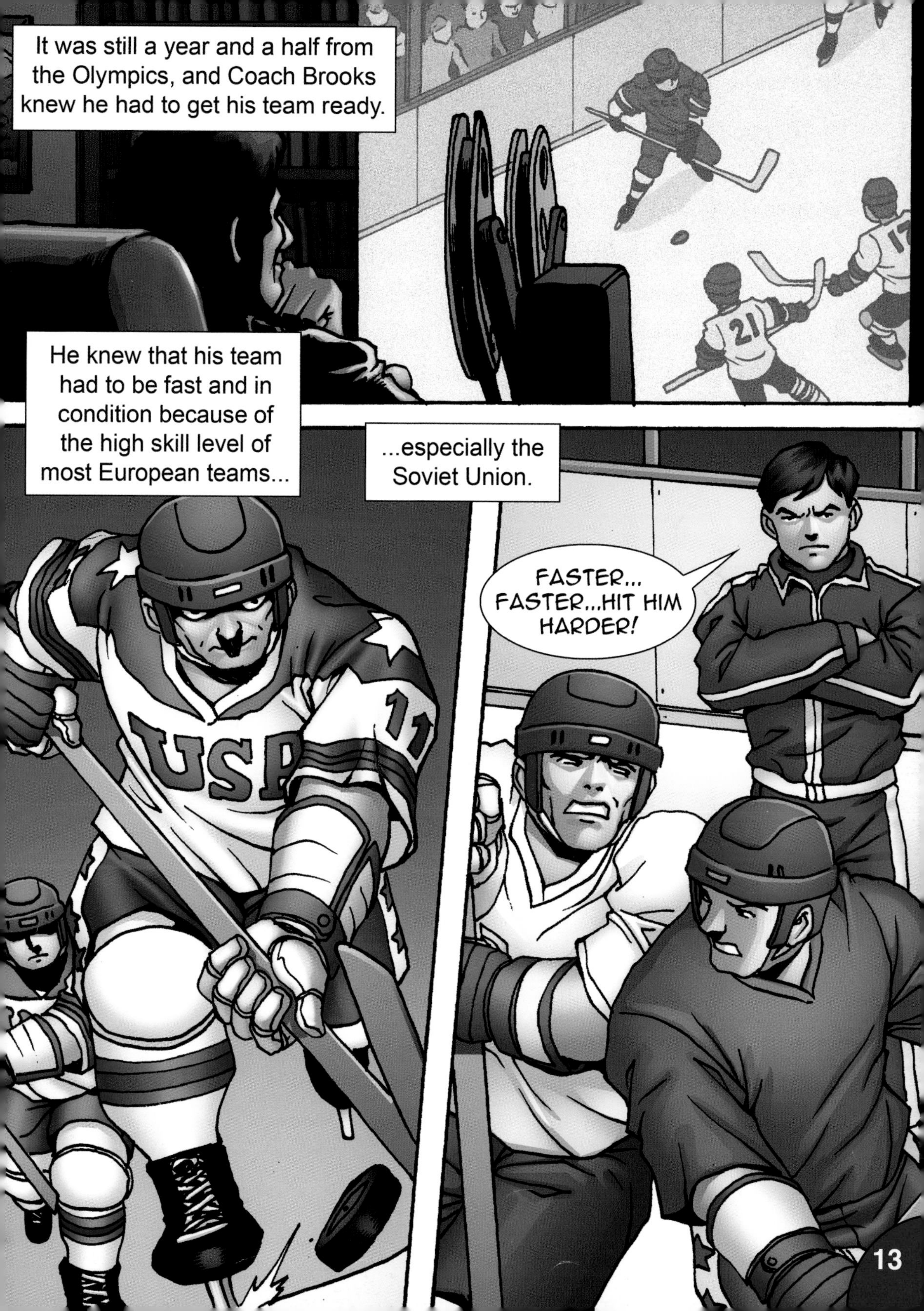

It was still a year and a half from the Olympics, and Coach Brooks knew he had to get his team ready.
He knew that his team had to be fast and in condition because of the high skill level of most European teams...
...especially the Soviet Union.
FASTER... FASTER...HIT HIM HARDER!
USA

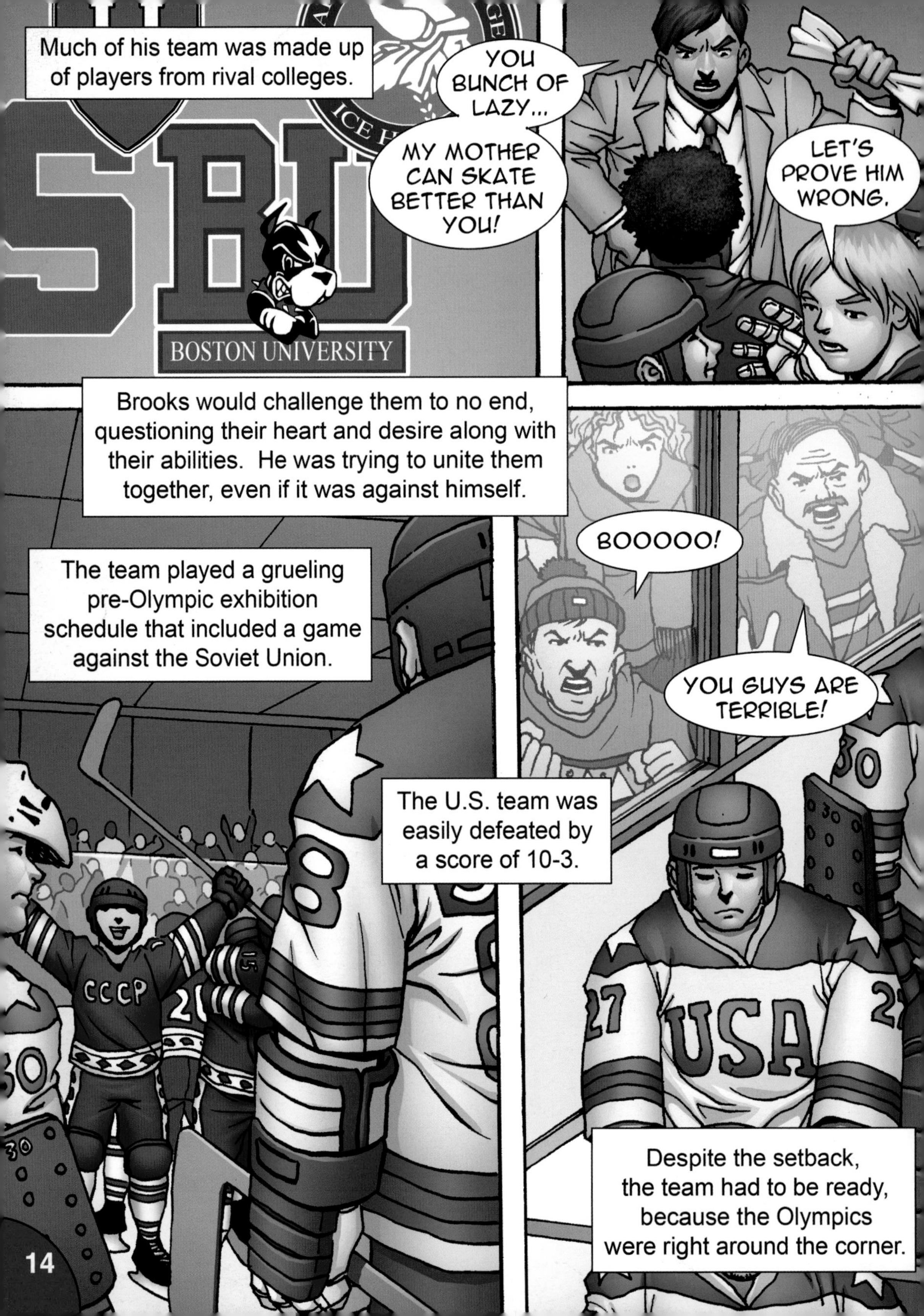
Much of his team was made up of players from rival colleges.
BOSTON UNIVERSITY
YOU BUNCH OF LAZY...
MY MOTHER CAN SKATE BETTER THAN YOU!
LET'S PROVE HIM WRONG.
Brooks would challenge them to no end, questioning their heart and desire along with their abilities. He was trying to unite them together, even if it was against himself.
The team played a grueling pre-Olympic exhibition schedule that included a game against the Soviet Union.
BOOOOO!
YOU GUYS ARE TERRIBLE!
The U.S. team was easily defeated by a score of 10-3.
CCCP
USA
Despite the setback, the team had to be ready, because the Olympics were right around the corner.

Chapter 3 Winter Games

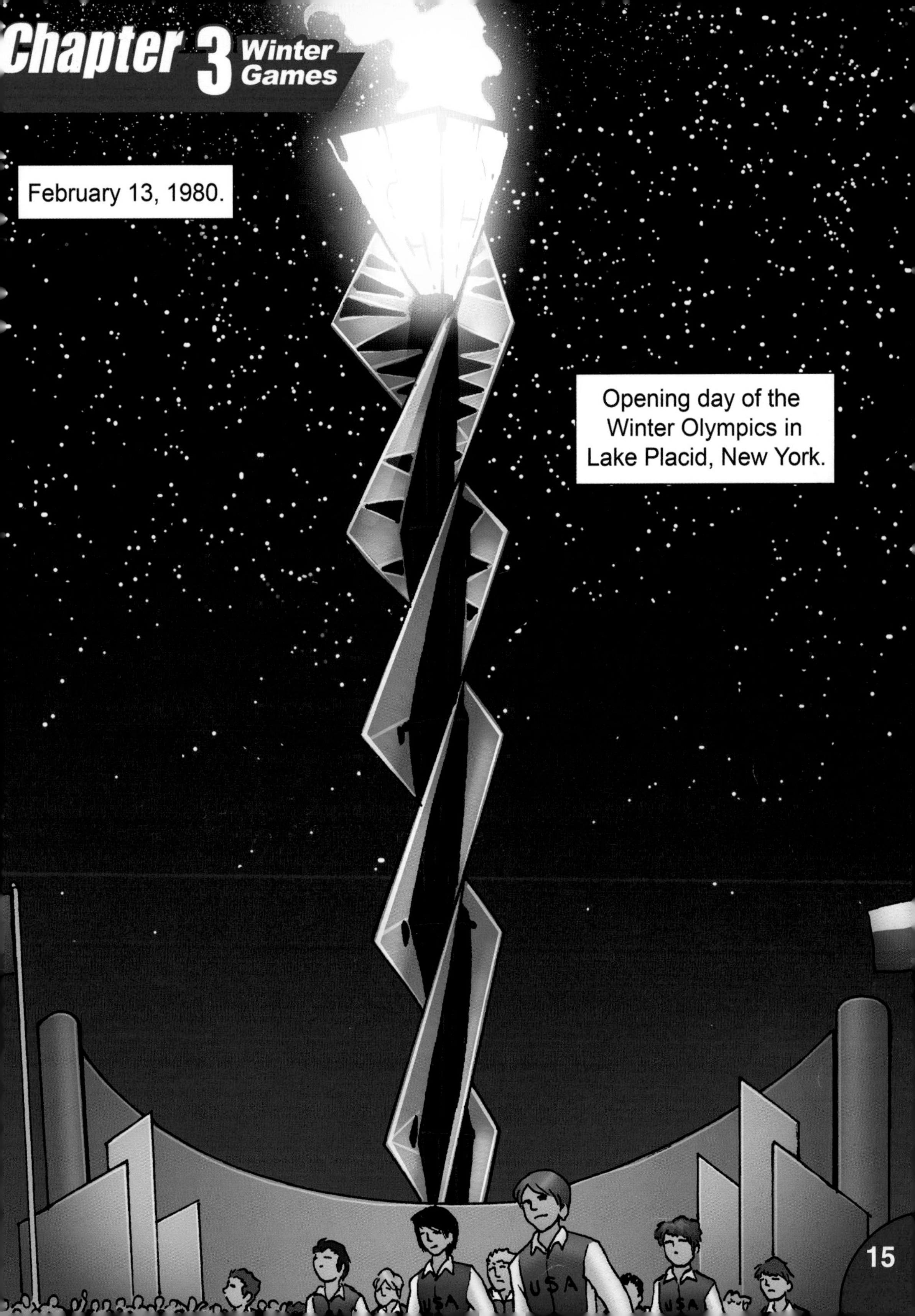
February 13, 1980.
Opening day of the Winter Olympics in Lake Placid, New York.
USA

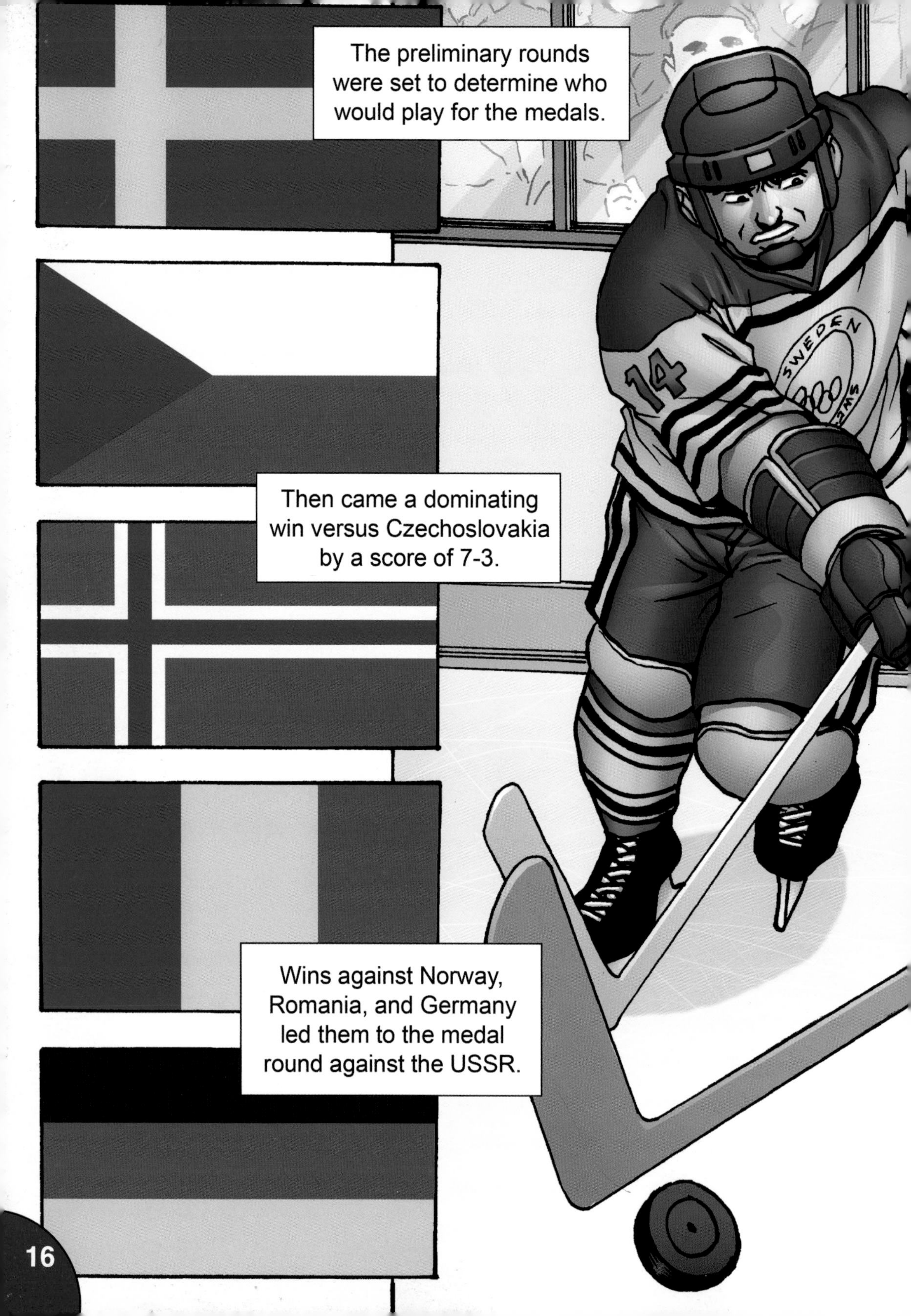
The preliminary rounds were set to determine who would play for the medals.
Then came a dominating win versus Czechoslovakia by a score of 7-3.
Wins against Norway, Romania, and Germany led them to the medal round against the USSR.
SWEDEN
14

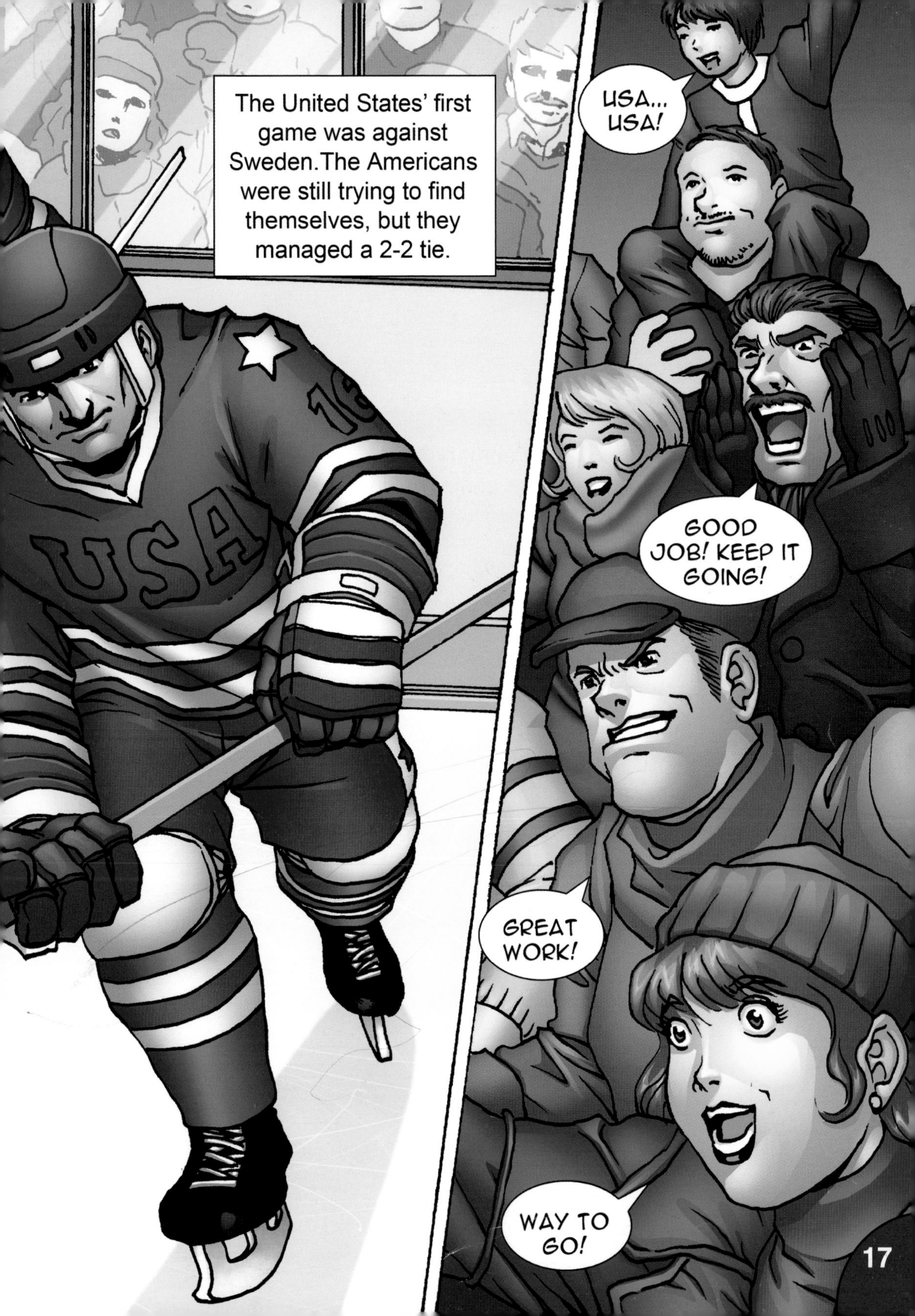
The United States' first game was against Sweden. The Americans were still trying to find themselves, but they managed a 2-2 tie.
USA... USA!
GOOD JOB! KEEP IT GOING!
GREAT WORK!
WAY TO GO!

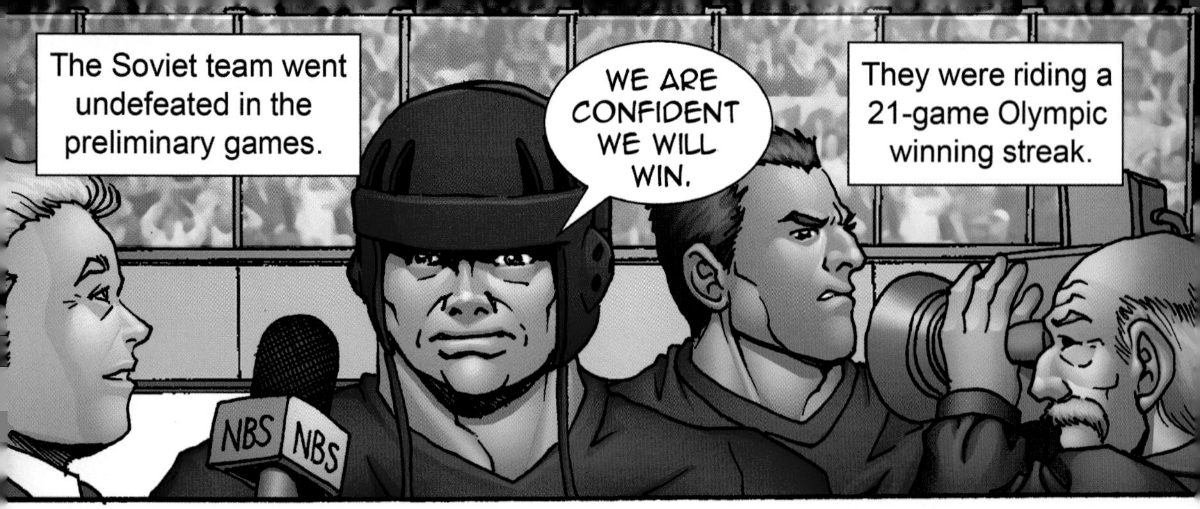
The Soviet team went undefeated in the preliminary games.
WE ARE CONFIDENT WE WILL WIN.
They were riding a 21-game Olympic winning streak.
NBS
NBS

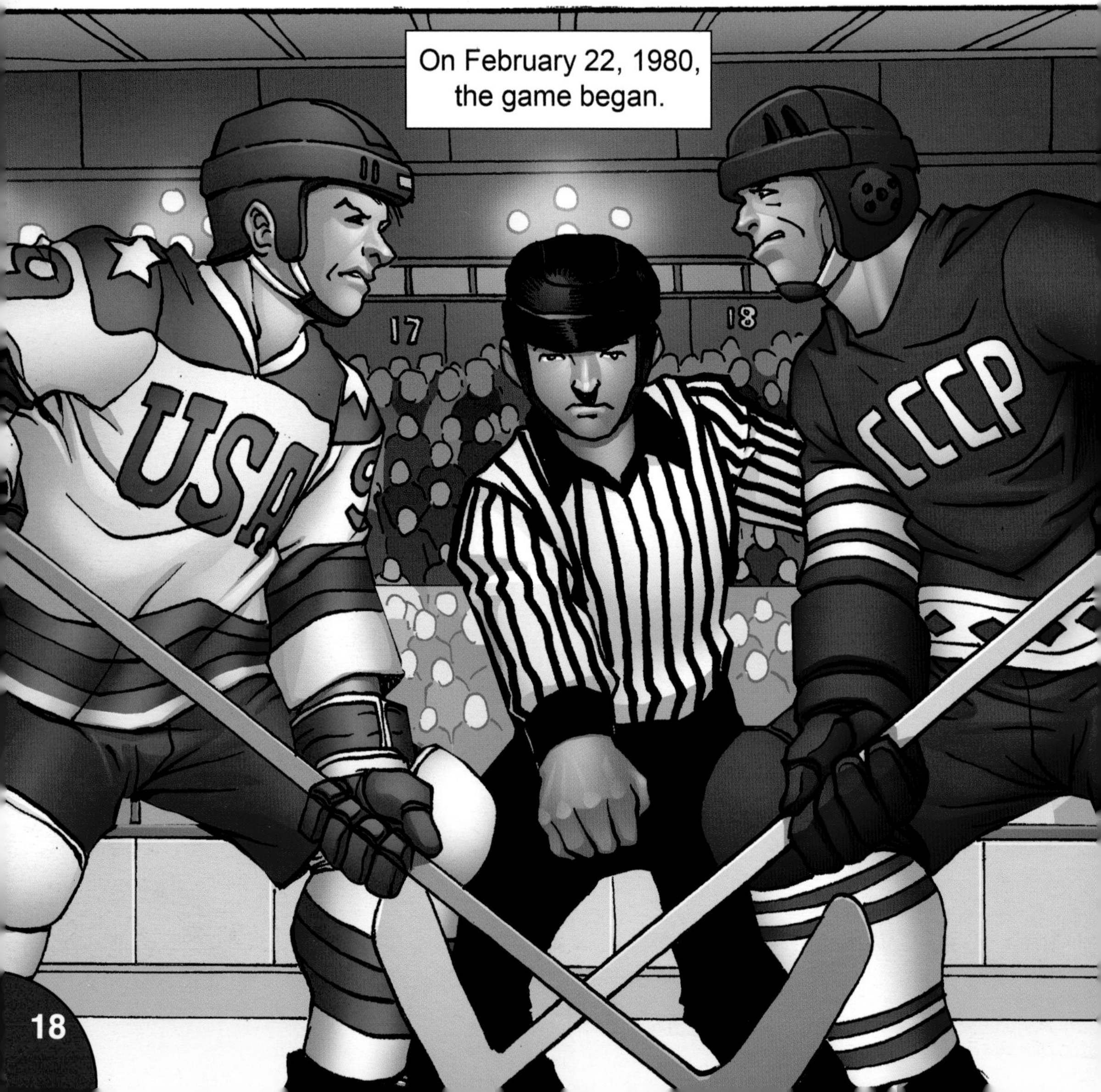
On February 22, 1980, the game began.
17
18
USA
CCCP

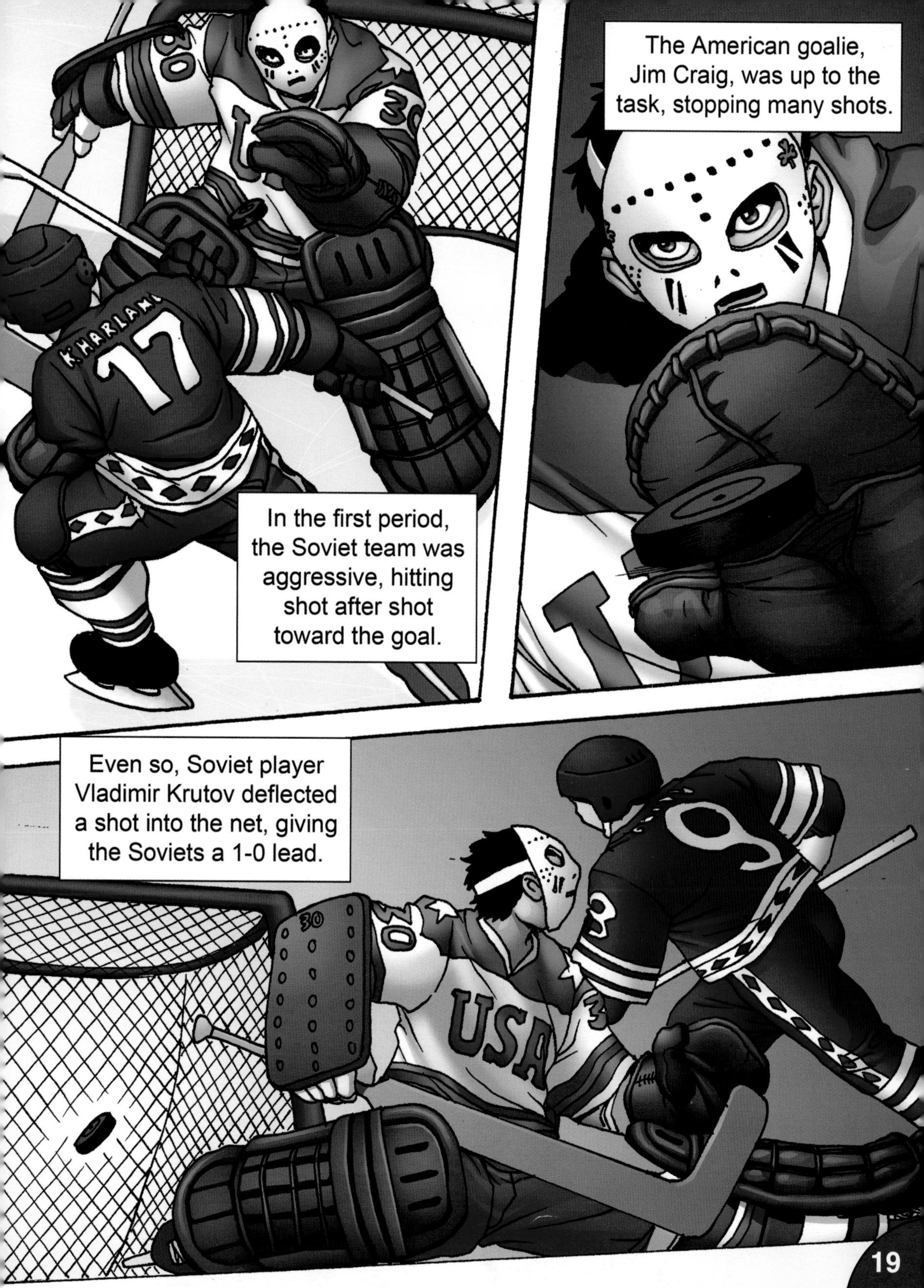
In the first period, the Soviet team was aggressive, hitting shot after shot toward the goal.
The American goalie, Jim Craig, was up to the task, stopping many shots.
Even so, Soviet player Vladimir Krutov deflected a shot into the net, giving the Soviets a 1-0 lead.
USA

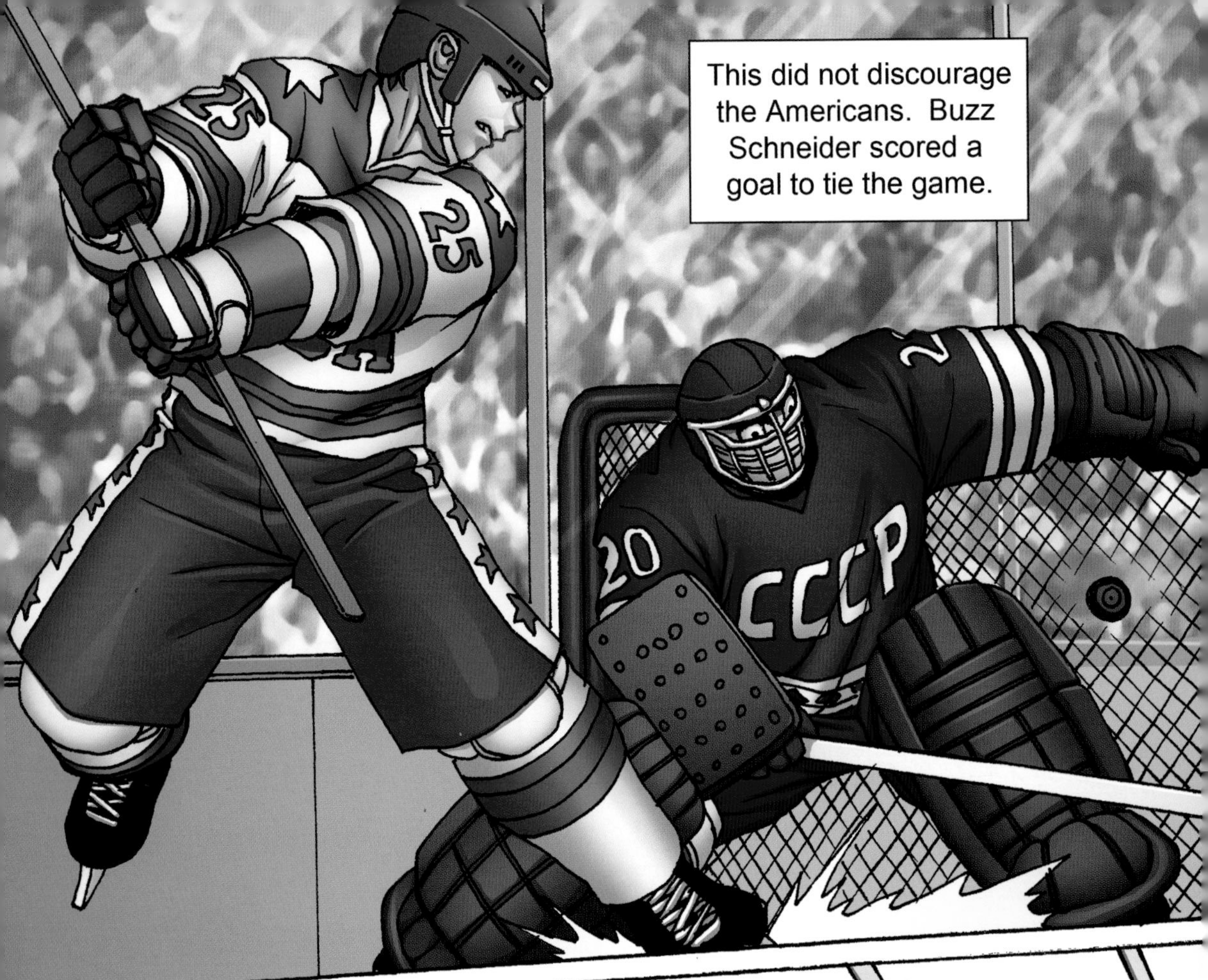
This did not discourage the Americans. Buzz Schneider scored a goal to tie the game.

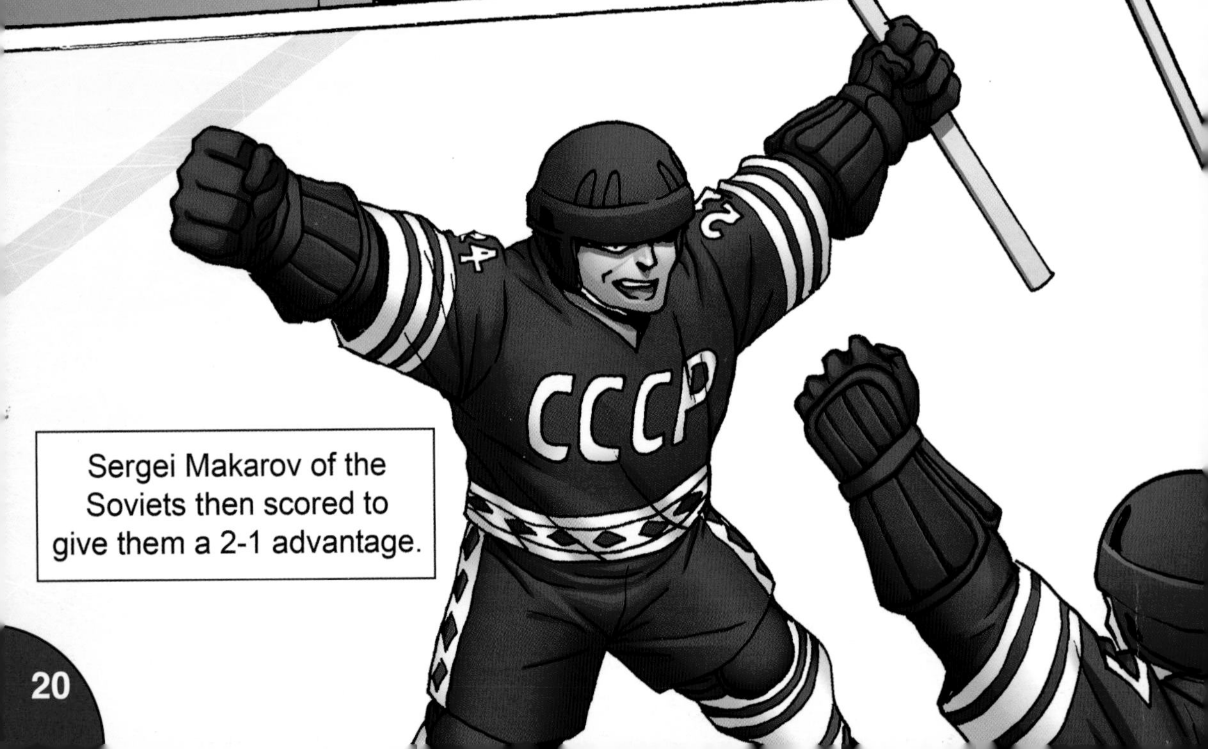
Sergei Makarov of the Soviets then scored to give them a 2-1 advantage.

Chapter 4 Tie Game

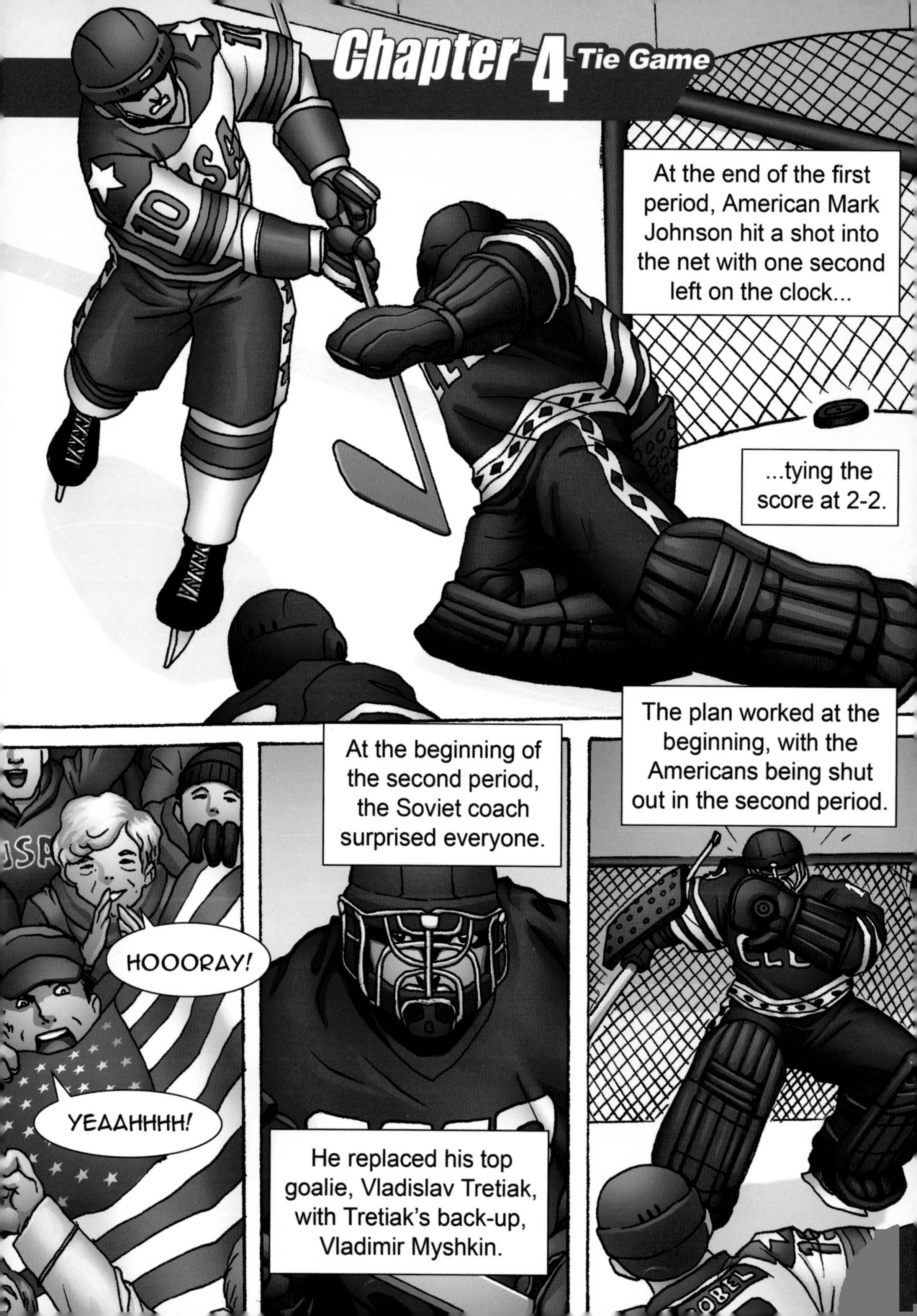
At the end of the first period, American Mark Johnson hit a shot into the net with one second left on the clock...
...tying the score at 2-2.
HOOORAY!
YEAAHHHH!
At the beginning of the second period, the Soviet coach surprised everyone.
He replaced his top goalie, Vladislav Tretiak, with Tretiak's back-up, Vladimir Myshkin.
The plan worked at the beginning, with the Americans being shut out in the second period.

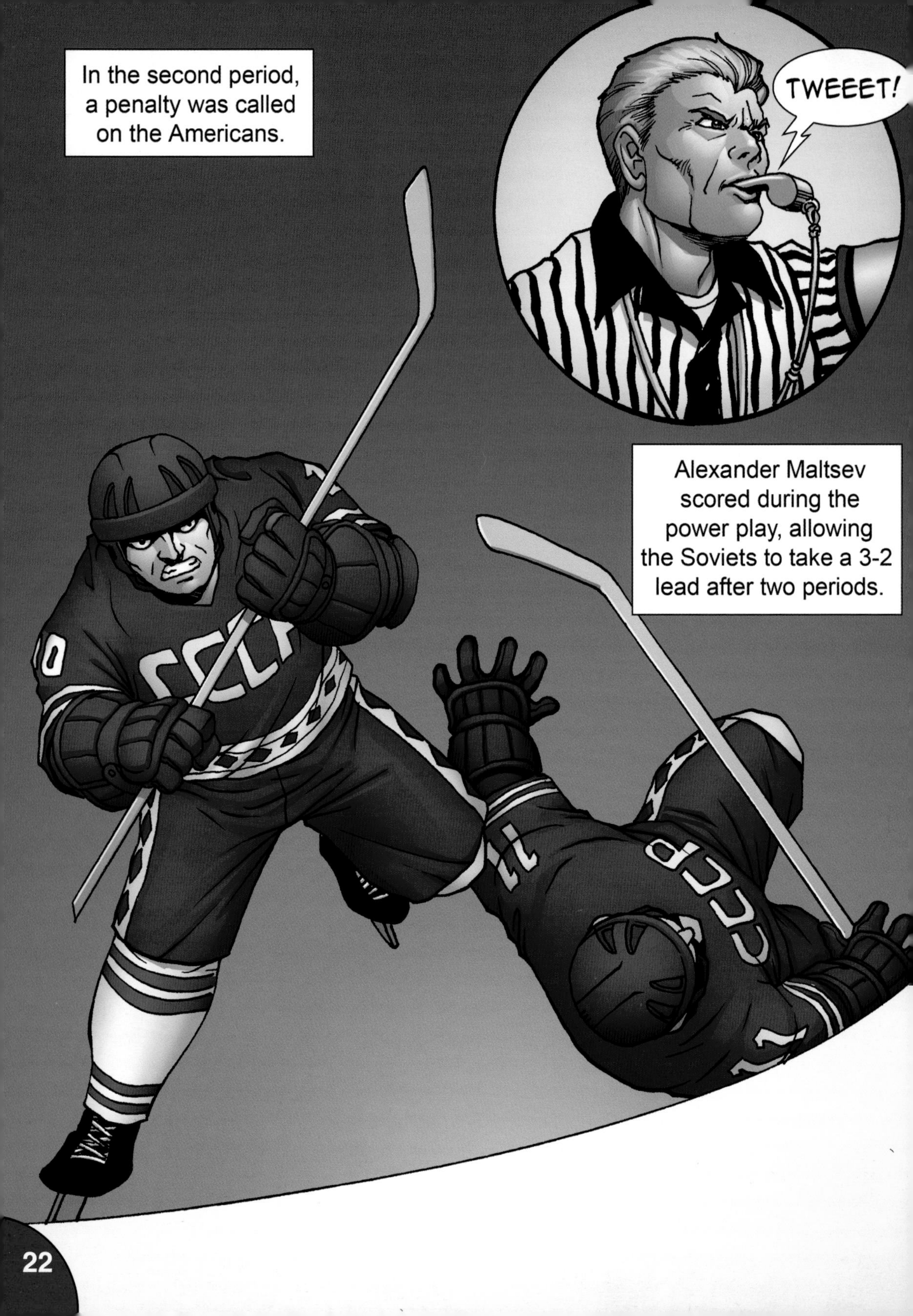
In the second period, a penalty was called on the Americans.
TWEEET!
Alexander Maltsev scored during the power play, allowing the Soviets to take a 3-2 lead after two periods.

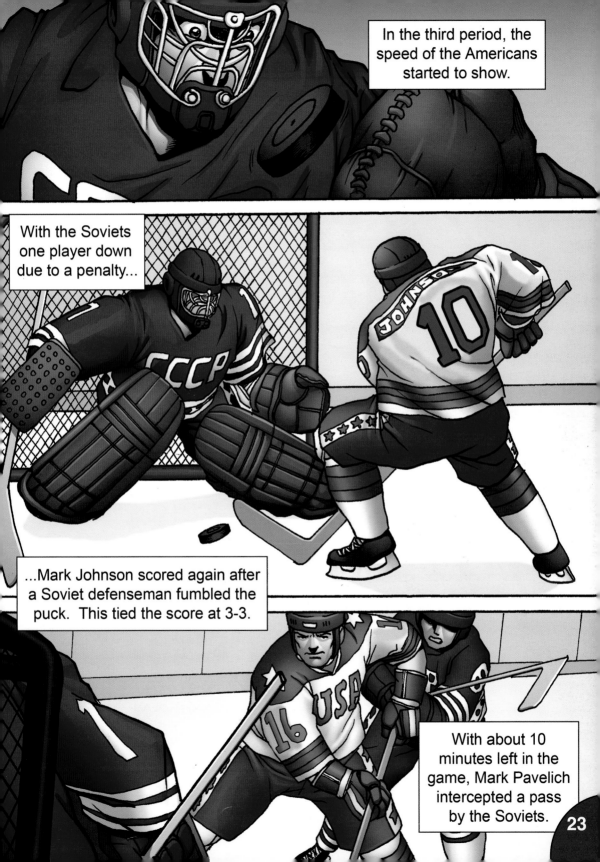

In the third period, the speed of the Americans started to show.

With the Soviets one player down due to a penalty...

...Mark Johnson scored again after a Soviet defenseman fumbled the puck. This tied the score at 3-3.

With about 10 minutes left in the game, Mark Pavelich intercepted a pass by the Soviets.

23

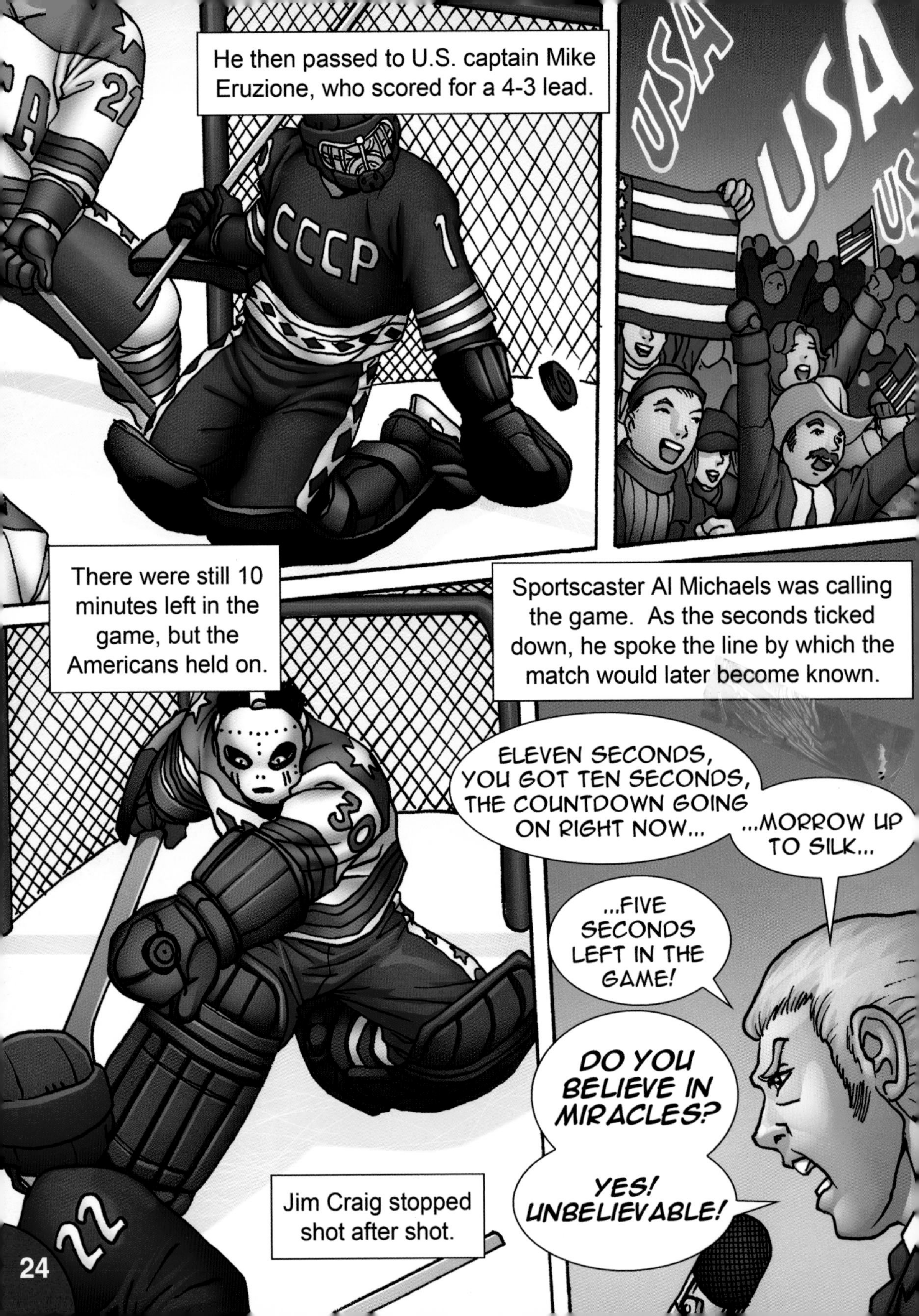
He then passed to U.S. captain Mike Eruzione, who scored for a 4-3 lead.
USA
USA
CCCP
There were still 10 minutes left in the game, but the Americans held on.
Sportscaster Al Michaels was calling the game. As the seconds ticked down, he spoke the line by which the match would later become known.
ELEVEN SECONDS, YOU GOT TEN SECONDS, THE COUNTDOWN GOING ON RIGHT NOW...
...MORROW UP TO SILK...
...FIVE SECONDS LEFT IN THE GAME!
DO YOU BELIEVE IN MIRACLES?
YES! UNBELIEVABLE!
Jim Craig stopped shot after shot.

Chapter 5 Victory

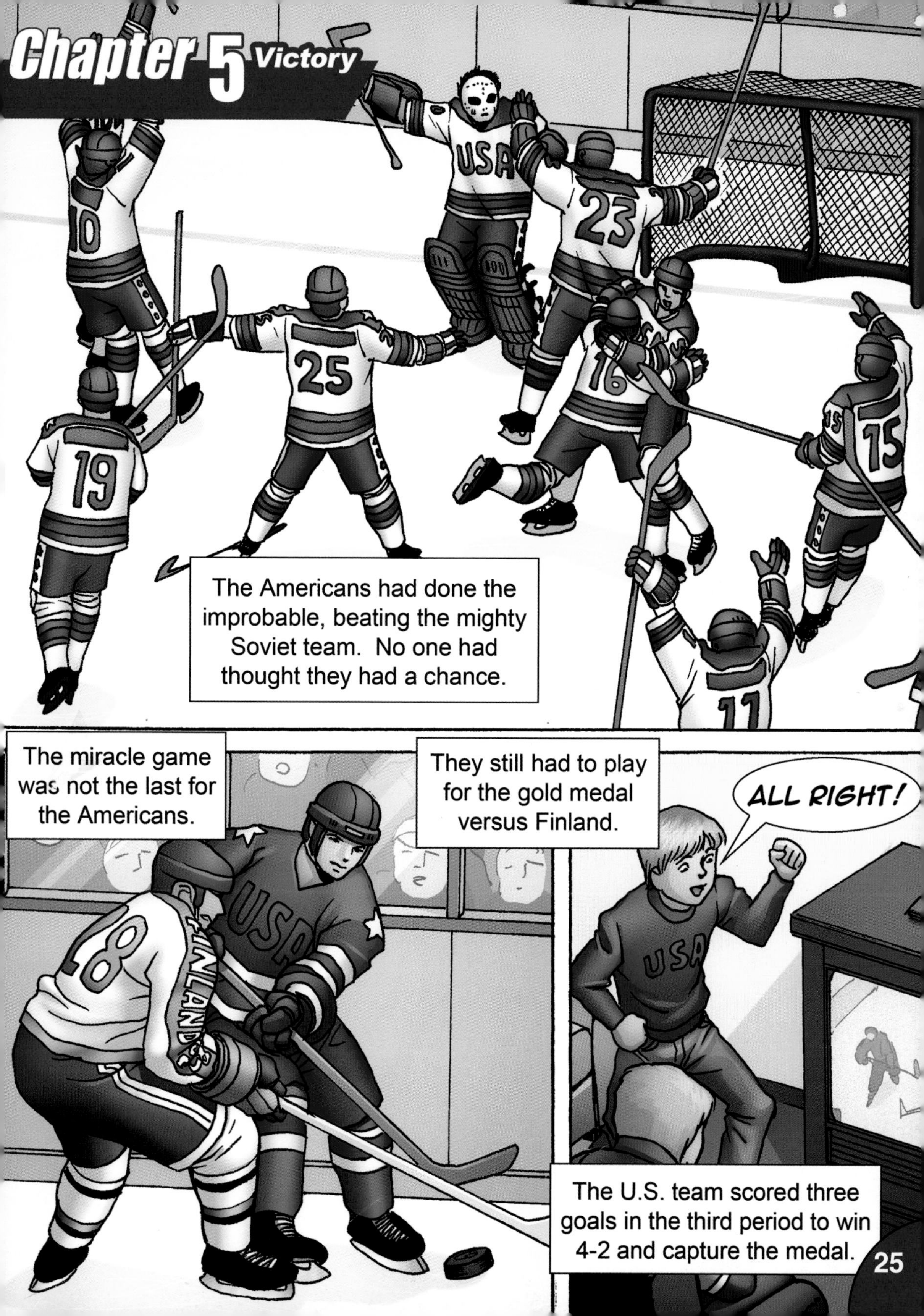

The Americans had done the improbable, beating the mighty Soviet team. No one had thought they had a chance.
The miracle game was not the last for the Americans.
They still had to play for the gold medal versus Finland.
ALL RIGHT!
The U.S. team scored three goals in the third period to win 4-2 and capture the medal.

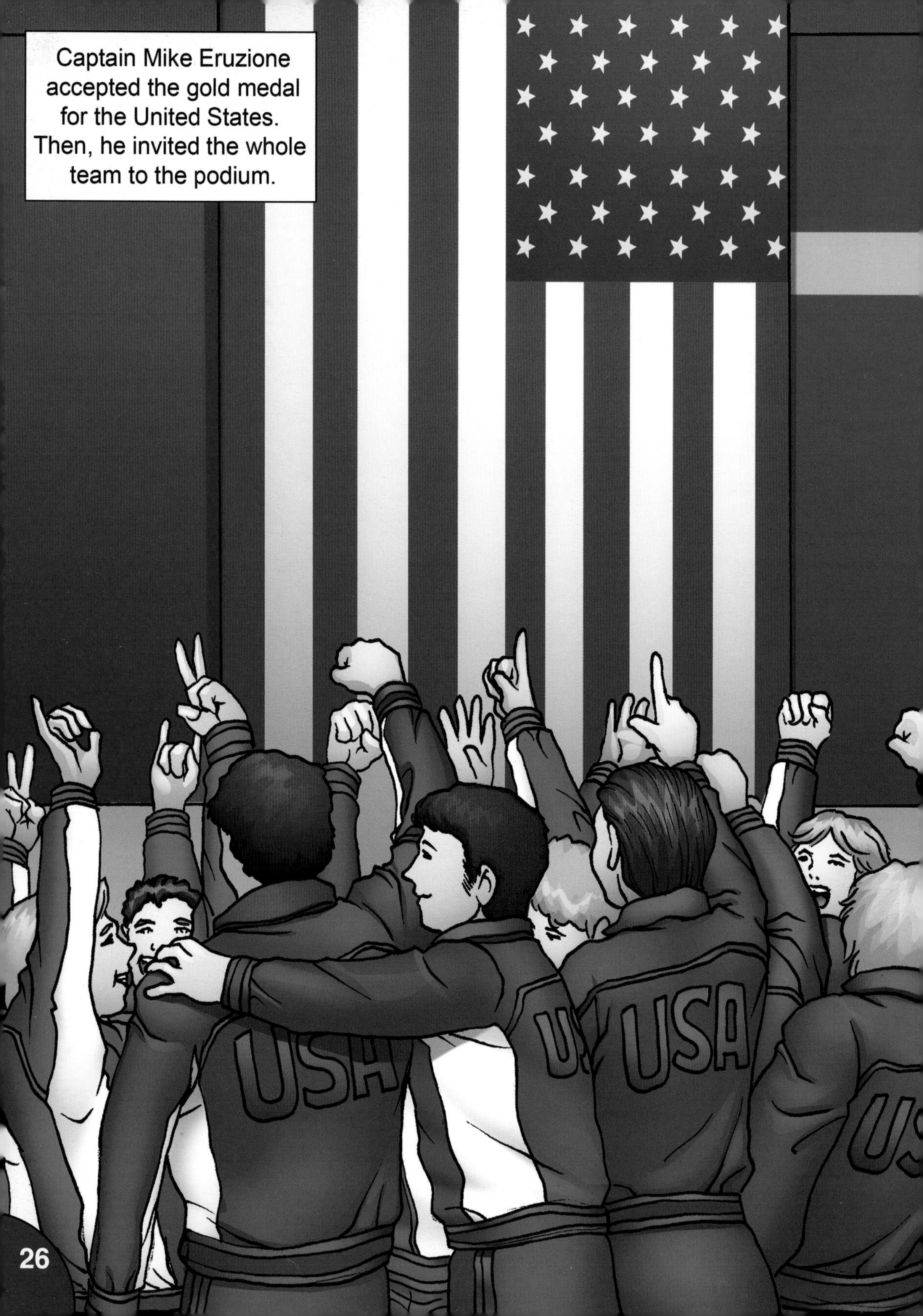
Captain Mike Eruzione accepted the gold medal for the United States. Then, he invited the whole team to the podium.
USA
USA

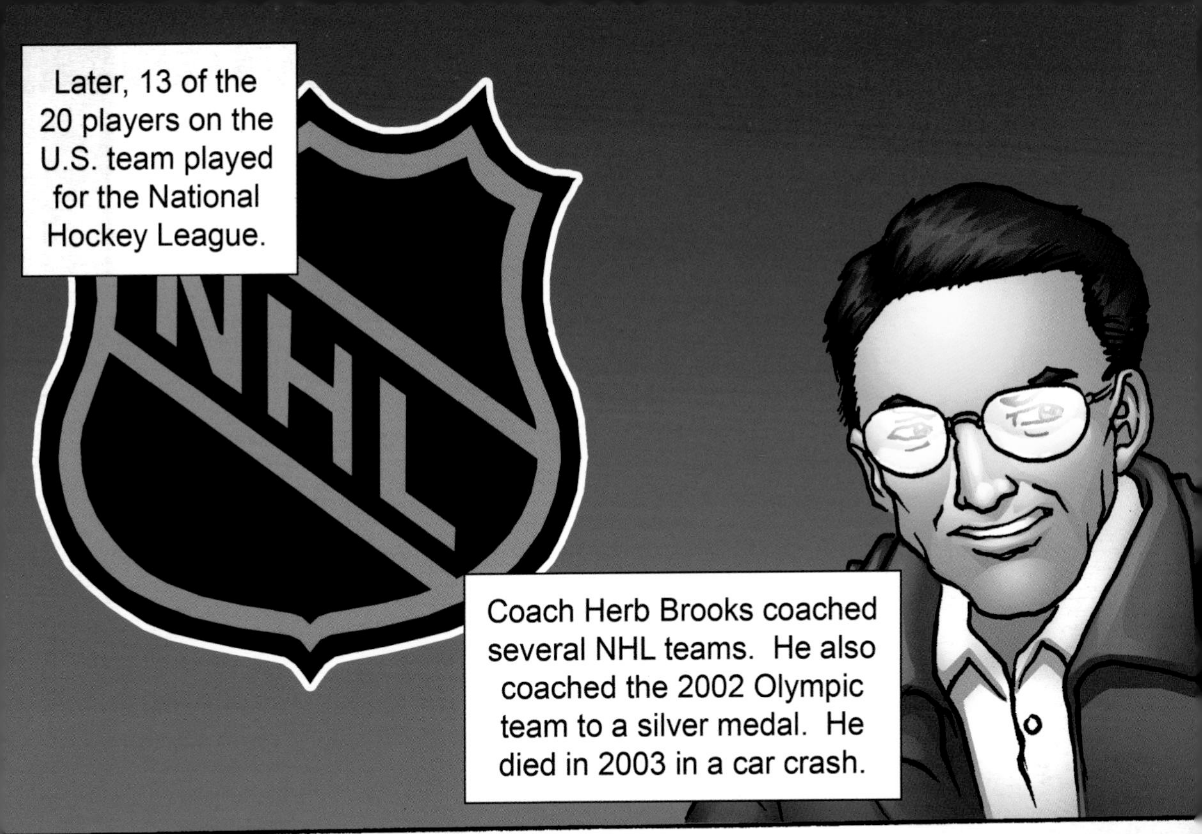
Later, 13 of the 20 players on the U.S. team played for the National Hockey League.
NHL
Coach Herb Brooks coached several NHL teams. He also coached the 2002 Olympic team to a silver medal. He died in 2003 in a car crash.

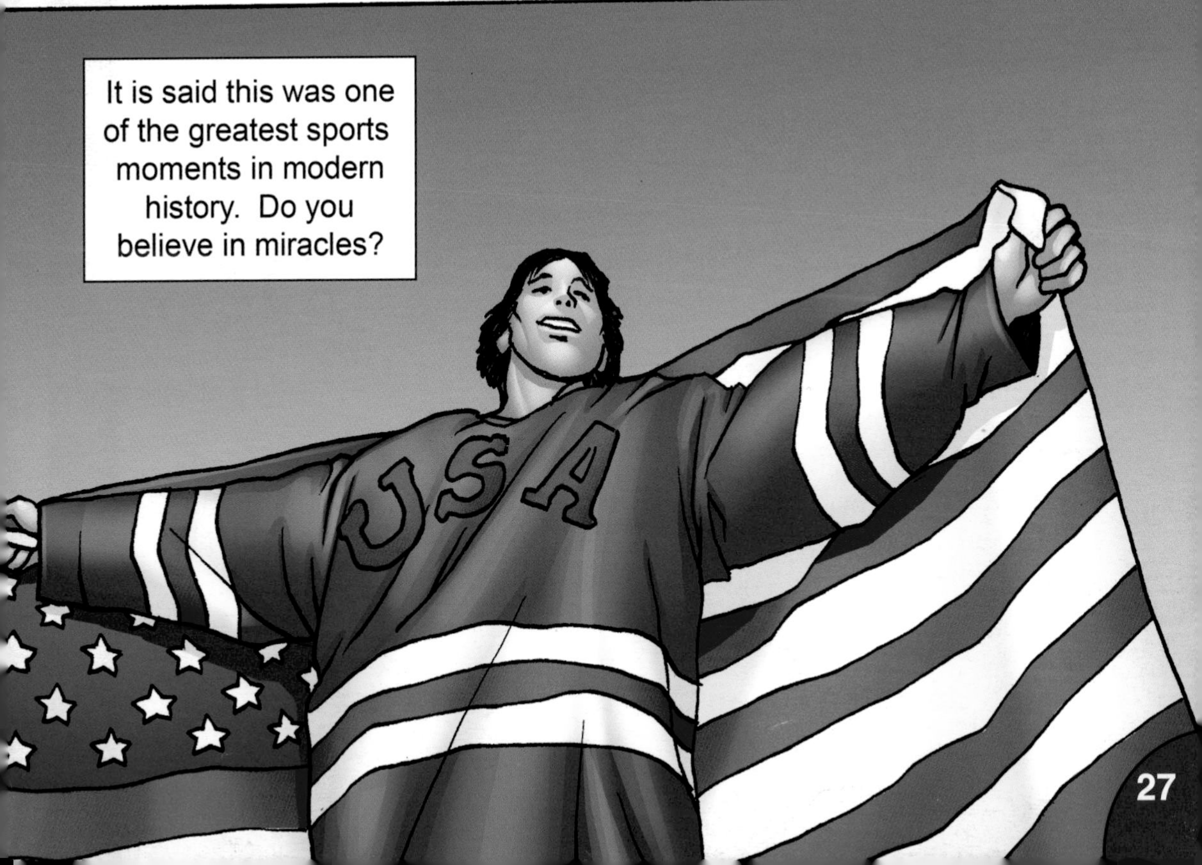
It is said this was one of the greatest sports moments in modern history. Do you believe in miracles?
USA

Timeline

1979 - The Soviet Union won the 1979 Hockey World Championship. The Soviet Union invaded Afghanistan in December.

January 1980 - President Carter started an embargo of goods to Russia.

February 9, 1980 - The USA hockey team lost an exhibition match with the Soviet Union 10-3.

February 13, 1980 - Opening ceremonies for the 1980 Winter Olympics were held at Lake Placid, New York.

February 13, 1980 - The USA hockey team tied Sweden 2-2.

February 14, 1980 - The USA hockey team defeated Czechoslovakia 7-3.

February 16, 1980 - The USA hockey team defeated Norway 5-1.

February 18, 1980 - The USA hockey team defeated Romania 7-2.

February 20, 1980 - The USA hockey team defeated West Germany 4-2.

February 22, 1980 - The medal round began. The USA hockey team defeated the Soviet Union 4-3 in what became known as the Miracle on Ice game.

February 24, 1980 - In the gold medal game, the USA defeated Finland 4-2 to win the Olympic gold medal.

1980 U.S. Olympic Hockey Team

#	Player	Ht.	Wt.	Birth	Hometown	College	Prev. Team
GOALTENDERS							
30	Jim Craig	6'1"	190	5/31/57	North Easton, MA	Boston Univ.	Boston Univ.
1	Steve Janaszak	5'8"	160	1/7/57	White Bear Lake, MN	Univ. of Minn.	Univ. of Minn.
DEFENSEMEN							
6	Bill Baker	6'1"	195	11/29/56	Grand Rapids, MN	Univ. of Minn.	Univ. of Minn.
3	Ken Morrow	6'4"	210	10/17/56	Davison, MI	Bowling Green	Bowling Green
17	Jack O'Callahan	6'1"	185	7/24/57	Charlestown, MA	Boston Univ.	Boston Univ.
5	Mike Ramsey	6'3"	190	12/3/60	Minneapolis, MN	Univ. of Minn.	Univ. of Minn.
20	Bob Suter	5'9"	178	5/16/57	Madison, WI	Univ. of Wisc.	Univ. of Wisc.
FORWARDS							
9	Neal Broten	5'9"	155	11/29/59	Roseau, MN	Univ. of Minn.	Univ. of Minn.
23	Dave Christian	5'11"	170	5/12/59	Warroad, MN	Univ. of ND	Univ. of ND
11	Steve Christoff	6'1"	180	1/23/58	Richfield, MN	Univ. of Minn.	Univ. of Minn.
21	Mike Eruzione	5'10"	185	10/25/54	Winthrop, MA	Boston Univ.	Toledo (IHL)
28	John Harrington	5'10"	180	5/24/57	Virginia, MN	Univ. of MN-Duluth	Univ. of MN-Duluth
10	Mark Johnson	5'9"	160	9/22/57	Madison, WI	Univ. of Wisc.	Univ. of Wisc.
24	Rob McClanahan	5'10"	180	1/9/58	St. Paul, MN	Univ. of Minn.	Univ. of Minn.
16	Mark Pavelich	5'7"	160	2/28/58	Eveleth, MN	Univ. of MN-Duluth	Univ. of MN-Duluth
25	William Schneider	5'11"	180	9/14/54	Babbitt, MN	Univ. of Minn.	Milwaukee (IHL)
8	Dave Silk	5'11"	190	1/1/58	Scituate, MA	Boston Univ.	Boston Univ.
19	Eric Strobel	5'10"	175	6/5/58	Rochester, MN	Univ. of Minn.	Univ. of Minn.
27	Phil Verchota	6'2"	195	12/28/56	Duluth, MN	Univ. of Minn.	Univ. of Minn.
15	Mark Wells	5'9"	175	9/18/57	St. Clair Shores, MN	Bowling Green	Bowling Green

General Manager:	KenJohannson/ Ralph Jasinski	Skating Coach:	DickVraa
Head Coach:	Herb Brooks	Physician:	Dr. V. George Nagobads
Ass't. Coach:	Craig Patrick	Trainer:	Gary Smith
Goalkeeping Coach:	Warren Strelow	Equipment Manager:	Bud Kessel

1980 USSR Olympic Hockey Team

#	Player	Position
1	Vladimir Myshkin	Goalkeeper
20	Vladislav Tretiak	Goalkeeper
2	Viacheslav Fetisov	Defenseman
5	Vasily Pervukhin	Defenseman
7	Alexei Kasatonov	Defenseman
12	Sergei Starikov	Defenseman
14	Zinetula Bilyaletdinov	Defenseman
9	Vladimir Krutov	Forward
10	Alexander Maltsev	Forward
11	Yuri Lebedev	Forward
13	Boris Mikhailov	Forward
16	Vladimir Petrov	Forward
17	Valery Kharlamov	Forward
19	Helmut Balderis	Forward
22	Viktor Zhluktov	Forward
23	Alexander Golikov	Forward
24	Sergei Makarov	Forward
25	Vladimir Golikov	Forward
26	Alexander Skvortsov	Forward

Head Coach: Viktor Tikhonov
Ass't. Coach: Vladimir Yurzinov

Glossary

aggressive - strong or intense behavior that is often hostile.

Cold War - a period of tension and hostility between the United States and its allies and the Soviet Union and its allies after World War II.

fumble - to lose control of an item while handling it or running with it.

grueling - long and difficult.

inflation - a rise in the price of goods and services.

intercept - to gain possession on an opponent's pass.

preliminary - something that comes before.

veteran - a person with a lot of experience.

Web Sites

To learn more about the miracle on ice, visit ABDO Publishing Company on the World Wide Web at **www.abdopublishing.com.** Web sites about the Olympic hockey team are featured on our Book Links page. These links are routinely monitored and updated to provide the most current information available.

Index

A
Afghanistan 5, 7

B
Brooks, Herb 9, 10, 13, 14, 27

C
Cold War 7
Craig, Jim 19, 24
Czechoslovakia 16

E
Eruzione, Mike 24, 26

F
Finland 25

G
Germany 16

I
Iran 5

J
Johnson, Mark 21, 23

L
Lake Placid, New York 15

K
Krutov, Vladimir 19

M
Makarov, Sergei 20

**Maltsev, Alexander 22
Michaels, Al 24
Morrow, Ken 24
Myshkin, Vladimir 21

N
National Hockey League 8, 27
Norway 16

P
Pavelich, Mark 23
preliminary rounds 16, 17, 18

R
Romania 16

S
Schneider, Buzz 20
Silk, Dave 24
Soviet team 8, 13, 14, 16, 18, 19, 20, 21, 22, 23, 25
Soviet Union 5, 7
Sweden 17

T
Tretiak, Vladislav 21
tryouts 10, 11

U
unemployment 5
University of Minnesota 9